The Challenge
of Cross-Border
Environmentalism

The Challenge of Cross-Border Environmentalism

The U.S.-Mexico Case

Tom Barry *with* **Beth Sims**
Foreword *by* **Dick Kamp**

No. 1 in The U.S.-Mexico Series

Resource Center Press
Albuquerque, New Mexico

and

Border Ecology Project
Bisbee, Arizona

First Edition, 1994

No. 1 in The U.S.-Mexico Series

Production/design by John Hawley/Resource Center Press

Resource Center Press
Box 4506 / Albuquerque, New Mexico 87196

Border Ecology Project
PO Drawer CP / Bisbee, AZ 85603

ISBN: 0-911213-45-7

Acknowledgments

This book would not have been possible without the direct contributions of many friends and colleagues. The staff of the Resource Center formed the foundation that allowed the book to take shape. Although all staff members helped at one time or another, especially important was the research assistance by Ricardo Hernández, Wendy Kappy, Erik Leaver, Laura Sheridan, and Steve Whitman; the administrative and personal support offered by executive director Debra Preusch; and the publications skills of production manager John Hawley. Vital in detecting errors, correcting misconceptions, and offering important insights were the following experts who commented on parts of the manuscript and shared their information: C. Richard Bath, Fernando Bejarano, Michael Gregory, Dick Kamp, Geoffrey Land, Nancy Lowrey, Stephen Mumme, and Angus Wright. We thank the many individual contributors and patrons of the Resource Center, and we gratefully acknowledge the financial support of the Jessie Smith Noyes Foundation for this publication, and of the Ford Foundation and the John D. and Catherine T. MacArthur Foundation for our U.S.-Mexico project.

It has been a great pleasure publishing the book with the Border Ecology Project, which through its own organizing and public policy work is successfully meeting many of the challenges of cross-border environmentalism.

Contents

What Border Environment?

I have always wanted to write a foreword to a book. Or one of those opening quotations that makes you wonder just where the author is going. The disjointed presentation that follows is my perception of border reality and most certainly is *not* indicative of the thoughtful, careful presentation of this book.

One recent week—here on the eastern Arizona-Sonora border—we were informed that the environmental side agreements to the North American Free Trade Agreement (NAFTA) were "complete." Shortly thereafter, as I accompanied my youngest daughter to her first day of kindergarten, a .38 slug flew by my ear and lodged in the wall of a class. Debris hit the five-year-old girl standing below me and two junior-high-school-age boys were arrested on charges of attempted murder. (They had been shooting from the top of a mining waste dump that may be partly responsible for an underground lake of pollution that is drifting south toward Naco, Sonora.) Authorities assured residents that the shooting was not connected to the recent series of AK-47–accompanied armed robberies in the nearby border town of Naco, Arizona. That crime spree spurred town residents—mostly Mexican American—to request that the Immigration and Naturalization Service (INS) install a metal wall (à la Tijuana/San Diego) along the town's Sonoran border to slow crime and flying bullets.

During this same week the INS announced that it would immediately be bringing building materials into Naco, Arizona, because of the "favorable" political climate. To the west, the city of Nogales had opposed a similar wall as a "fascist" act and nearby Douglas, Arizona, was hotly divided over whether a wall should be built. It's not surprising that the Mexican municipal presidents of all the border towns found the fence insulting. (It should be noted here that Douglas and its sister city Agua Prieta, together with Naco, Arizona, and Naco, Sonora, are economically dependent on the drug trade.) For my part, I limited my involvement to a call for an environmental impact statement (EIS) with respect to the potential impact of the border wall on surface and groundwater flows, the movement of wildlife, and on this transboundary society (basing my petition on arguments similar to those that led to the June 1993 court decision requiring the Clinton administration to conduct an EIS on the NAFTA). An EIS is needed whether or not such an "iron curtain" along the border is racist, oppressive, protective, or all of the above.

As I write this, I am trying to puzzle out just *what* is that black smoke rising up from the desert to the east of Naco, Sonora? Yet I'm not sure I really want to know. But such things are part of my job as director of a nonprofit border environmental organization.

Some eighty miles west of here in Ambos (both) Nogales Arizona-Sonora, a sad fracas continues. A Mexican-American cancer victim in Nogales, Arizona, has drawn attention to the inordinately high number of lupus and cancer cases in the city. The dying man believes the disease clusters are the result of pollution from Sonora. Clearly there is a south-north flow of contaminants, including a copious stream of air pollution as well as nitrate- and solvent-contaminated groundwater and sewage that cross the international border. Major suspects behind some of the industrial water pollution are unidentified U.S.-owned maquiladora plants located on the Mexican side. As a result of a locally initiated binational study, it's well known that in Nogales, Sonora, various squatter communities that get water trucked to them are drinking known and suspected carcinogens from a contaminated well located along the Arroyo Nogales.

The efforts of the cancer patient to document the presence of environmental disease in Nogales have drawn the attention of University of Arizona medical professionals and public health activists. They have volunteered thousands of hours to survey the communities on both sides, and in the process they are gaining the cooperation of concerned Sonorans as well as of the officials and residents of Nogales, Arizona.

Unfortunately, the cancer victim-activist blames the Mexican side a priori for the disease clusters. Feeling personally victimized, he refuses to join in any cooperative investigative effort with his ancestral compatriots due to their "totally corrupt" system. He is also the leader of the Nogales "build the metal wall" movement.

Furthermore, he believes that the university researchers are selling out the community by working with the Mexicans and by claiming it could take five years to complete a cancer study. Strangely, an antiwall and longtime Nogales, Sonora, community activist has joined him in denouncing both the University of Arizona and Mexican academic efforts to study the cancer cluster. Venom and confusion are carrying the day.

The result is bitterness and paralysis among victims and researchers alike. Since most cancer epidemiological studies result in indeterminate conclusions and little action, Nogales' attempt to isolate a problem and its causes faces great odds. The worst enemies of these border cities, however, appear to be the fears, distrust and prejudice of their own residents—or, even worse, self-prejudice fed by pain and desperation.

The University of Arizona researchers and the Sonoran community activist (a single mother of eight children), who has joined in maligning them, are all people who have selflessly dedicated their lives to improving the lives of others. I know them all well. None of this dissension makes sense. Yet on a human level there does exist a certain logic: The border residents are living and working within a disorder that corrupts any hope that you can control events and improve life. Paranoia joins with poverty, corruption, and idealism to boil up a poisonous brew.

Border environment, to answer the opening question, is the whole binational and bicultural ambience—or *ambiente*, in Spanish. Environment is the drug trade, the disease, the poverty, the pollution, as well as the attitudes of the population and the government(s).

All is not darkness and despair, or many of us would leave. Much of the nonurban area around here is stunning: 10,000-foot peaks with Douglas Fir and Aspen trees rising from high desert and oak foothills. Ancient haciendas—and marijuana plantations—are tucked into mountains and valleys graced by small rivers and hot springs. All this within a hundred miles, and closer than the modern western sprawl of Tucson. Naturally, the land is a treasure. The mines, smelters, maquiladoras and the skyrocketing growth of the border cities with their industrial contamination and open sewers came later.

"He who fears corruption fears life," wrote community organizer Saul Alinsky; Tobias Wolfe opened up his beautiful autobiography *This Boy's Life* with the same quote.

Many who live along the border understand that mixed in with the sleaziness of the region's economy and politics and the Mexican government's Alice in Wonderland bureaucracies (now decentralizing into what seem to be thousands of fragments) is an unusual sense of freedom. This feeling is a product of the local blend: the relative wealth of the U.S. borderlands and the implicit belief in manifest destiny and a sense of order found on the U.S. side mixed with Mexican humanism, humor, fatalism and basic human kindness. In spite of the obstacles involved in building cross-border alliances to solve some of our environmental (in the *ambiente* sense) problems on both sides of the border comes the realization that—especially within Mexico where the rules are still not defined—all things may be possible. Remarkably this sense of freedom persists despite the heavy police presence that dominates the U.S. side of the border.

You see and live a dichotomy here: seeming pie-in-the-sky visions of trade agreements that embody a new world order of controlled economic development and new wealth (albeit at poverty wages on the Mexican side) while the state government of Sonora has just been ordered to cut all agency budgets by 50 percent—a stark warning of deep budgetary trouble in Mexico.

Longtime border residents know that no central governmental policy will solve the problems of the border region or of Mexico in general—real solutions can only grow out of the local communities themselves. Examples are abundant, but here's a particularly disgraceful one: After more than ten years of the La Paz border environmental agreement, there is still no "official" public data on groundwater quality on the Mexican border released by the EPA and its counterparts in Mexico within SEDESOL. We talk about billions needed for border infrastructure and environment, yet for perhaps a half-million bucks we could have had some decent baseline information about the poisons people do or don't drink. In Nogales, the information that we do have was locally generated and that, folks, is typical for the border region.

Making political solutions reflect complex personal and human realities is an eternal struggle; the borderlands are no different. By accepting what many trade promoters and border congressional representatives will not—that there will be no free lunch in resolving border regional social problems— we could see positive change in the region. Those who are making the money through trade and investment in this low-wage economy must pay: through user fees, cross-border tariffs, or whatever other schemes might work. They need to pay for the cancer studies, for the clean water in Nogales, for the hazardous waste dumpings of past and present, as well as for the social stress that rapid development brings.

No other sector has paid or will pay: Nobody wants to buy municipal bonds to pay for the cleanup of waste quagmires and for marginal homes for poor people who will never generate the income to pay taxes. Schemes to invest in border environment will be limited to those public works (such as water, sewage, garbage, and middle-income housing projects) that can make some money. I have estimated that the cost of living in nearby Agua Prieta, Sonora, is 90 to 110 percent that of Douglas, Arizona, its sister city. The average maquila wage is around five to six dollars a day. The average wage for a laborer within the narcotics industry—albeit inconsistent—is estimated to be twenty times that of a maquila worker.

What are some conclusions that we might draw from my ramblings here? That new schemes for planned social development and pollution prevention and cleanup with strong local control are needed with substantial funding generated by local employers and investors—because we have no tax base. That crime will continue to pay in the near future. That experimentation in new social projects must be mixed with trust among locals—a trust that is fragile even among friends. Finally, as John Muir and others have said, that all acts are interconnected.

The environmental side agreements to the NAFTA (which may be a dead issue by the time you read this) are an incomplete start to providing some creative new frameworks that could work with or without a NAFTA. The provisions eliminating any jurisdiction of the new Commission for Environmental Cooperation over natural resources are particularly unsettling. As is the fact that plans relating to development and foreign exploitation of agriculture, mining, forestry, and maritime enterprises cannot be challenged.

Then again, that kid would probably have shot at me no matter how the NAFTA side agreements turned out. To be honest, most of us working binationally on environmental and health research and advocacy will probably continue working much as we have, NAFTA or no NAFTA.

Now to this book. The Resource Center has long dived head first into the personal lives of citizens in North and Central America to document conditions and propose solutions to many social problems. Their *Country Guides* to Central America have become essential reading to those seeking accurate synopses of political and economic conditions. During the Reagan years in particular, the Resource Center was often the only group that could unravel the conservative individuals and institutions that seemed to freely mix governmental influence and policy creation with "disinterested" nonprofit research. For the past four years, the Border Ecology Project (BEP) has worked with the authors and their staff in many locations within northern Mexico and on the U.S. side of the border. The multicultural staff of the center has understood not only the subtleties of Mexican and U.S.-Mexico politics, but has also understood the constraints on people's lives, and in a truly balanced and sympathetic way has explained the human context for policy needs.

BEP is proud to copublish *The Challenge of Cross-Border Environmentalism* and to support the good work of the Resource Center in this small way. This is a unique book in its tying together of many threads empirically to make an argument that the small-scale models forming at the grassroots level—combined with progressive binational policies—could provide a basis for sustainable development in the border region.

Many of these citizens groups not only work within the system, they also recognize that there is little choice but to try to do the job that governments do not, and simultaneously to try to persuade the governments to institutionalize their own monitoring, right-to-know, and pollution exposure practices. Increasingly, environmental and health advocates in the border region understand that their local problems and solutions are linked to much larger policy issues. *The Challenge of Cross-Border Environmentalism* is an important contribution to understanding the struggles that these people face.

Dick Kamp
Bisbee, Arizona
25 August 1993

The Lesson
of the Cobalt Man

Vicente Sotelo Alardín sits in a Juárez prison, accused of a theft that triggered one of the border's worst environmental catastrophes. More than 4,000 people were exposed to high levels of radioactive cobalt 60 from a cancer-therapy machine taken in 1983 from the Medical Center for Specialities in Ciudad Juárez.[1] Like many other border incidents, the causes and the repercussions of the cancer-therapy machine "theft" were not isolated to one side of the international border. Described as the worst radiation disaster in North America, the cobalt 60 incident in Juárez was truly an international affair.[2]

While working as a hospital custodian/electrician, Sotelo claims he was told by his supervisor to dispose of some unused equipment that was languishing in a hospital warehouse. One of the pieces of junk he carried away to the Yonke Fénix junkyard was a twenty-year-old radiotherapy machine that the hospital had purchased secondhand in the United States but had never used.

Loaded with the cobalt 60 isotope, in the form of some 6,000 pellets each the size of a pinhead, the machine was used by the Methodist Hospital in Lubbock, Texas, to burn away cancers. Although the use and transfer of such nuclear devices are strictly regulated in the United States, international sales are not monitored. In this case, U.S. brokers were not required to notify the nuclear authorities of the Mexican government nor did the deal require a check on the competence or the licensing of the purchaser. In selling the cancer-therapy machine to a doctor at a Juárez hospital, X-Ray Equipment Company of Fort Worth violated no U.S. rules—even though a similar sale to an unlicensed purchaser would have meant a fine or a jail sentence in the United States.[3]

After collecting dust in the hospital storeroom for six years, the device was hauled away to a Juárez junkyard that later sold the machine along with other scrap metal for recycling by two steel foundries, one of which is a subsidiary of a St. Louis company. Mixed in with other metal, the pellets contaminated thousands of steel rebar (used to reinforce concrete) and furniture parts that were subsequently manufactured with recycled metal. Because the device was partially dismantled before arriving at the junkyard, an unknown quantity of the metal pellets spilled out of Sotelo's truck, contaminating various sections of Juárez.

Five weeks after Sotelo dropped off the machine at Yonke Fénix the same cobalt 60 isotope set off alarms at the Los Alamos National Laboratories near Santa Fe, New Mexico. A driver for the Smith Pipe & Steel Company of Albuquerque made a wrong turn when making a delivery at the nuclear weapons research center, and the contaminated steel rebar triggered the center's radiation detector, thus beginning an international effort to track down and retrieve all the deadly steel. Radioactive rods and metal furniture were eventually recalled from twenty-three states and four other countries including Mexico.

Mexican officials calculated that close exposure to the cobalt 60 would be equivalent to absorbing 35,000 chest X rays. One junkyard worker has already died from a rare bone cancer, and others have suffered from sterility and skin discoloration. Apparently feeling that someone had to take the blame for the catastrophe, Mexican authorities eventually decided to arrest Sotelo for theft. By mid-1992 Sotelo had been waiting a year and a half for his case to come before a judge. The hapless Sotelo—whom prison guards call *El Cobalto* (the Cobalt Man)—charges that the Mexican government is using him as a scapegoat.

Sotelo's story mixes personal tragedy, startling coincidence, and social injustice. But perhaps more than anything it highlights the many noneconomic implications of unregulated cross-border trade. The fate of the Cobalt Man highlights the close links between the public health and environmental future of the two neighboring nations.

With or Without NAFTA

The environmental and health repercussions of U.S.-Mexico relations along the border are the main focus of this book. The disposal of industrial wastes, air and water pollution, threats to occupational and public health, loss of flora and fauna, and ineffective environmental regulation along the border serve as a vivid regional portrait of the ecological and health problems resulting from increasing economic integration. With or without NAFTA, it is likely that this integration of trade and investment will deepen.

But these and other similar problems extend far beyond the borderlands. The increasingly close economic relations between the United States and Mexico raise new questions about the compatibility of development and the environment. Mexico, like most countries, has long favored economic development at the expense of environmental quality. Beginning in the late 1980s, environmental initiatives by the Mexican government indicated a new ecological sensibility, at least in terms of public discourse. At the same time, however, the government's drive to deregulate the economy and the urgency with which it has sought to attract foreign investment raise concern that environmental protection will continue to take a backseat to economic stimulation. Underlining this concern was a 1992 World Bank report that stated that "Mexico suffers from grave environmental problems exacerbated by several decades of industrialization without assessment of, or attention to, environmental costs."[4]

Although the industrial development of the Mexican borderlands does serve to illustrate many of the environmental consequences of liberalized trade and investment, questions about the environmental sustainability of development are not peculiar to the border.[5] For the most part, both nations still fail to account for the environmental and health repercussions of growth when calculating the effects of increased trade and investment no matter where they occur.

For its part, the United States has been pushing Mexico since the early 1980s to adopt a more open economy and give a freer rein to foreign investment with little regard to the environment. Although the United States has advocated that Mexico adopt U.S.-style environmental regulations, it has largely ignored that Mexico has neither the funds nor the political will to enforce such rules.

Certainly the Mexican government, business community, and citizenry bear primary responsibility for the environmental degradation caused by Mexico's past and present development policies. But in this epoch of economic integration, responsibility must also be shared by the United States, which stands in a better position to guide the forces of global integration. Unfortunately U.S. economic policies tend to aggravate Mexico's environmental crisis. Left out of binational negotiations are such matters as the environmental effects of increased oil exports to the United States and the restructuring of Mexico's food system—both of which Washington has been advocating. Also explicitly omitted have been any controls over "natural resource harvesting" such as mining, forestry, water exports, and the use of agricultural land.

The lack of environmentally conscious economic planning is perhaps most apparent in the ongoing reform of the agricultural sector. As Mexico opens its domestic market to U.S. grain imports and seeks to increase its share of the U.S. market for fruits and vegetables, it has failed to consider the health and environmental costs of this integration of regional agricultural markets.

Since the 1950s Mexico has promoted horticultural exports to the United States, using subsidized water and energy to underwrite the agroexport industry. Trade liberalization and changes in Mexico's agrarian reform have increased the incentives for U.S. agribusiness to transfer production and packing operations south of the border. But like the western United States, Mexico will soon have to confront the environmental costs—contamination caused by pesticide and fertilizer runoff, the draining of underground aquifers, erosion, and salination of irrigated lands—brought on by modern agribusiness. Whether Mexico can afford to continue subsidizing basic energy and water costs of these large export operations, which in many cases are controlled by such transnational corporations as Del Monte and Unilever, is another question that has not yet been answered.

Mexico's gradual switch to a trade-based food policy—depending on cheaper food imports to substitute for beans and corn produced by the peasantry—also has untold environmental consequences. As imported basic grains and the elimination of state protection undermine traditional peasant agriculture, rural-urban migration will grow, compounding the environmental crisis facing an increasingly urban Mexico. Economic crisis in the countryside at the same time will probably escalate soil erosion and deforestation as desperate peasants seek to eke out livings on marginal lands. In this way, the specter of poverty-induced ecocide in rural Mexico looms ever larger.[6]

With or without a formal free trade accord, economic integration means rising threats to Mexico's environment in other sectors as the country opens up to foreign investment and pushes export production. After a decade of declining investment in the petroleum industry, increased onshore drilling threatens the Lacondon tropical forest in southeastern Mexico and stepped-up offshore drilling in the Bay of Campeche further endangers the fisheries and the marine environment. Indicative of the fundamental lack of environmental consciousness on the part of both the U.S. and Mexican trade officials was the section on petroleum and energy of the proposed NAFTA accord in which the term *environment* was not mentioned once. New foreign investment in the country's mineral reserves represents another potentially adverse environmental repercussion of Mexico's trade and investment liberalization.

The environmental effects of free trade, whether it be with Mexico or any other nation, extend far beyond issues of hazardous waste disposal, pollution-haven investment, or cross-border pollution. Without proper management, economic integration has profound environmental and social implications.[7] Free trade can mean increased natural resources harvesting as consumers in industrial countries can better access the timber, mineral, petroleum, seafood, plant, and agricultural resources of less developed nations. Without controls, demands of northern consumer demands for such tropical products as shrimp could quickly deplete Mexico's reserves. By affecting international commodity trade, the liberalization of international trade can radically alter agricultural production. Rural women and the poor are often the first victims of this shift from basic foods production to agroexports because they lack the resources to adapt to new market conditions.

The negative consequences of free trade may be somewhat balanced by removing subsidies to U.S. agricultural producers, thereby cutting back on overproduction. At the same time, however, cutting farm subsidies may also mean that government funding to promote proper soil conservation will be threatened.[8]

Achieving sustainable development is becoming the most important challenge for industrialized and underdeveloped nations alike. Considering the increasing fragility of transborder ecosystems and the toll that unregulated economic growth takes on public health and welfare, the environmental and social costs of development can no longer be ignored.

In this era of global communication, financial, and production systems, crossing international borders comes easily to investors and traders. Yet just as national political boundaries do not make economic sense to the proponents of free trade, neither do borders have much meaning for environmentalists interested in conserving and rehabilitating ecosystems. Measures to protect one nation's environment do little good if companies can simply cross borders to avoid those regulations.

The chapters in this part of the book point to the wisdom of environmentalists who have long insisted that ecosystems and environmental contamination extend across international boundaries. Together the following chapters on ecological deterioration, air and water pollution, hazardous dumping, and pesticide poisoning paint a grim picture of ecological devastation. But there is a positive side, too. A new international environmental consciousness is developing as community leaders, government bureaucrats, and social justice activists from Mexico and the United States come together to work out common solutions. No longer isolated on the radical fringe of the environmental movement, the concept of sustainable development has moved into the center of the debate over the future of regional economic integration.

Chapter 1

The Nature
of the Borderlands

The lack of water defines the border's natural environment. From east to west along the boundary, the aridity of the surrounding region is its most striking feature.[9] The semiarid grassland steppes of the Rio Grande Valley along the Texas border give way to the unforgiving Sonoran desert of the Arizona and California border. Rising above the hot and arid lowlands are the "mountain islands" that are the southern extensions of the Rocky Mountains, offering cooler temperatures and high forest vegetation. The summer heat is intense but is relieved in most parts by "monsoons" that sweep across the desert skies in August.

Availability of water was the most pressing issue facing the Southwest's earliest developers. Theirs was not an environmental concern about how best to conserve scarce resources. Rather, they rushed to divvy up the water among the most powerful private and public players. Not until the last few decades has the use of nonrecharging groundwater reserves become a contentious development issue. With wells drying up or becoming contaminated, the residents of the borderlands are realizing that finite groundwater resources also impose severe limits on future growth.

Quantity, of either surface water or groundwater, is just one part of the region's water crisis. Also critical is declining water quality. Above and below the ground, water has become dangerously contaminated with human, agricultural, and industrial wastes.

Desert Rivers

Two main river systems unite—and divide—the United States and Mexico: the Rio Grande and the Colorado River. Descending from the eastern slopes of the Continental Divide in southeastern Colorado, the Rio Grande slices through New Mexico before reaching the Mexican border at El Paso. For 1,264 miles the river or the riverbed defines the border. The flow of the Rio Grande disappears in the desert sand at Fort Hancock and does not appear again for fifty more miles until it receives the waters of the northbound Río Conchos. Finally the Rio Grande trickles into the Gulf of Mexico. Early explorers, approaching the river from different directions, believed the 1,800-mile river—the fifth longest in North America— was actually several different waterways. Seen from the Gulf, it was labeled the Río de las Palmas (river of palms), and from the south it was christened the Río Bravo del Norte (fierce river of the north), the name of honor it still holds in Mexico.[10]

The Colorado River, which springs to life in the 14,000-foot peaks of Wyoming and Colorado, forces its way through the most arid expanses of North America, plunging 2.5 miles on its 1,450-mile path to the Gulf of California. The only major source of water between the Rocky Mountains and the Sierra Nevada, the Colorado River marks the entire Arizona-California line but defines the international boundary for only twenty-four sandy miles. This mighty river, which carved the Grand Canyon and turns the turbines of more than thirty hydroelectric plants, crosses into Mexico a defeated, lifeless stream. During its trip to Mexico the Colorado River is tripped up by ten major dams and straitjacketed to serve the manifold demands of rural and urban communities in the otherwise waterless expanses of the Southwest.

The Colorado and Rio Grande share common lifelines. One on the east side of the Continental Divide and the other on the west, the two rivers are conceived on the snow-capped peaks in the Rockies. They are mighty rivers, pushing their way past formidable natural barriers and giving life where there is no other. But their power has been sapped and their beauty scarred by the ranchers, farmers, miners, and urban developers who have claimed the rivers as their own. Despite their magnificent beginnings, the Rio Grande and Colorado River come to tragic ends. So depleted is the Rio Grande by the time it reaches Brownsville-Matamoros that the salty waters of the Gulf of Mexico now wash into its shallow channel. More shameful still is the fate of the Colorado, whose waters in most years do not even reach the Sea of Cortez. Instead, its brackish remains simply disappear into the burning sands of Sonora. And the Cucapá Indians—the "river people"—who once depended on its flow into the gulf no longer have a river to fish in or call their own.[11]

The two rivers have long been central elements in U.S.-Mexico relations. As might be expected, sharing the rivers in these scorched borderlands has not always been easy—or equitable. To a large extent, the law of the strongest has prevailed. Mexico's relative lack of technical expertise and economic resources have historically placed the country at a disadvantage in claiming its water rights.[12] The asymmetry in U.S.-Mexico relations has in the case of water rights been aggravated by the different geographic positions of the two nations as upstream and downstream riparians. Nonetheless, international water agreements have been hammered out that have proved to be models of bilateral resource management. The joint International Boundary and Water Commission (IBWC), which has been managing boundary and surface water disputes along the border since 1889, has succeeded in resolving most disputes in an amicable fashion.[13] But the challenges over water use and quality now facing the two nations are daunting.

Disputes over the international sharing of the Colorado River and Rio Grande date back at least to the 1870s.[14] Tensions have also arisen over the use and abuse of the waters of lesser waterways, such as the San Pedro River that originates by the mining complex in Cananea, the Santa Cruz River Basin in the twin cities of Nogales, the New River that flows north from Mexicali, and the Tía Juana (or Tijuana) River that laces into Southern California.

Faced with the rapid development of the Southwest, the United States took the lead in shaping the course and distribution of the Colorado River. In 1922 the states bordering the river signed the first interstate compact regulating the Colorado. The agreement specified that the flow of the river would be divided equally between the upper and lower basins, with the midpoint being Lees Ferry in northern Arizona.[15] Recognizing that Mexico had some claim on the Colorado, the Interstate Compact of 1922 specified that Mexico would receive the surplus over the 16.9 million acre-feet (maf) that was tentatively allocated between the upper and lower basins. (One acre-foot is the quantity of water needed to cover an acre with one foot of water.) But the river's average flow was grossly inflated, having been based on an extremely wet period, with the mean average flow probably some 2 maf less than the original optimistic calculation.[16] Furthermore, if no surplus was available, the compact provided that the burden of supplying water to Mexico would be shared equally by both basins.

More than two decades later an international treaty stipulated just how much water Mexico was entitled to.[17] It was agreed that Mexico would annually receive at least 1.5 maf—about 10 percent of the Colorado River's flow—except in years of extreme drought, and that the IBWC would be the implementing agency. At least for a couple of decades the treaty eased tensions between the two countries over water allocation. But the treaty was silent on the issues of water quality and on the pumping of transboundary groundwater aquifers—the very issues that later emerged as the most prominent concerns on both sides of the border.

Most early tensions over water in the borderlands were over the sharing of surface water, not over its quality. But because of the rising salinity of the Colorado River water delivered to Mexico, the quality of surface water became a major international issue in the 1960s.[18] The Colorado is naturally a highly saline river, and as it descends toward Mexico its salinity increases dramatically. Before all the major economic development in the southwestern states, the river's salinity would naturally rise from fifty parts per million (ppm) in Wyoming to about 400 ppm at the border. As the water became increasingly used and reused on its journey toward Mexico, its salinity upon reaching the border more than doubled, regularly reaching at least 800 ppm. This increased salinity became a new irritant in border relations.

In 1961 the salinity of the water moving into the Mexicali Valley became so extreme that the Colorado River water delivered to Mexico proved disastrous to the valley's agricultural production.[19] The sudden increase in salinity that year, caused by the release of highly saline groundwaters into the international stream by the U.S. Bureau of Reclamation's Wellton-Mohawk Irrigation Project east of Yuma, eventually forced Washington to intervene. After twelve years of debate and minor adjustments a definitive solution was reached in 1973 in which it was agreed that the water delivered to Mexico must be of approximately the same quality as U.S. users receive.[20] The agreement was the result of Mexico's formal protest to the U.S. government, its threat to take the matter to the World Court, and President Echeverría's announcement that the salinity crisis was his country's leading bilateral priority. Instead of closing down the responsible irrigation project, Washington sought another solution. The Nixon administration turned to the Bureau of Reclamation—the government agency dubbed the Bureau of Wrecklamation by many environmentalists for its habit of damming and channeling rivers.

In its continuing effort to keep western farmers and ranchers happy while not egregiously violating agreements with Mexico, the Bureau of Reclamation constructed a large desalination plant near Yuma, Arizona. Rather than restricting use of the Colorado's waters to comply with the 1944 and 1973 accords with Mexico, the U.S. government spent some $260 million for a plant to treat the highly saline water from the Wellton-Mohawk Irrigation Project. But after a dozen years under construction, the finally completed Yuma desalination plant is now regarded more as a white elephant than as a credible solution to the Colorado River's salinity. Politics, not practicality, dictated the creation of the plant, which will cost $38 million annually to operate. Once regarded as the state of the art in reverse-osmosis desalination, the Yuma plant was technologically obsolete even before it came on line in 1992.[21] This technological solution to the problems created by the Wellton-Mohawk Irrigation Project is just one of many federal projects that have dipped into U.S. tax revenues to subsidize the wasteful and exorbitantly expensive irrigation of the desert lands of Southern California.[22] It would have been much less expensive for the government simply to buy out the water rights of the Wellton-Mohawk than to build the desalination plant. But the powerful agricultural lobbies and their attacks on anyone challenging the prevailing system of federal subsidies of western agriculture kept other solutions to the water crisis from being seriously considered.[23]

Notwithstanding the contribution of the Yuma desalination plant, high salinity continues to aggravate cross-border tensions. As the end of the pipeline, Mexico suffers disproportionately from the salinity of borderland waters. In a classic case of trying to solve one problem only to create another, the brine from the Yuma desalination plant flows to the Santa Clara Slough and upper gulf waters in Mexico, damaging a natural habitat for many birds, fish, and dolphins.[24] Salinity, however, is a major concern along both sides of the border. The Bureau of Reclamation estimates that the nine million tons of salt flowing down the Colorado River have caused $311 million in annual damage in the lower basin because of increased treatment costs, crop loss, and corrosion of water-handling facilities.[25] As historians can attest, salinity can have calamitous consequences not just for farmers, but for entire societies. Largely because of salt accumulation in the soil, for example, the Sumerian civilization of ancient Mesopotamia collapsed.[26] The economic boom of the borderlands does not yet show signs of decline, but the region does seem to be reaching the limits of development, as evidenced by available water resources and the decreasing quality of what little water there is. If current trends continue, the salinity of the Colorado River will reach 1,150 ppm by the year 2010, spelling the death of agriculture in the Mexicali and perhaps even the Imperial Valley.[27] Because of the burst of population growth and the increased energy development in the region, it is becoming ever more difficult to control salinity. Despite an array of engineering and conservation measures implemented by the IBWC and affected local governments, the crisis persists. In fact, the Texas Water Commission warned the Environmental Protection Agency (EPA) that unless salinity levels dropped along the Rio Grande, not only will crops face ruin but saline water may also threaten the maquila industry which depends on good-quality water.[28]

Groundwater Conflicts

The one case that may best illustrate the complexity and inherent tensions of transboundary water sharing is that of the All-American Canal, which transfers Colorado River water into the Imperial and Coachella valleys of California. The canal, and its history, also represent the asymmetry and lack of parity between the two international neighbors. The All-American Canal was preceded by another canal with a similarly pretentious name, the Imperial Canal. Early developers of the Imperial Valley decided that it would be much easier to move the water they needed through a dry riverbed in Mexico than to attempt to construct a channel through the Yuma Sand Hills, which separated the river from the valley.

In typical fashion the developers found a Mexican willing to lend his name to the project, thereby giving it legal standing in Mexico. It also helped that this *prestanombre* (name lender), Guillermo Andrade, was a relative of dictator Porfirio Díaz. The Imperial Canal was a great success in that it not only provided irrigation waters to California but also opened up the Mexicali Valley for agricultural development. It was not, however, Mexicans who benefited, but rather U.S. investors, such as Harry Chandler of the *Los Angeles Times*, who together with other investors in the Colorado River Land Company bought up 800,000 acres of the Colorado River delta land in Mexico.[29]

Accumulated silt deposits and poor river management laid waste to the Imperial Canal in 1906 when a flood changed the course of the river, resulting in extensive crop and home damage on both sides of the border. It was then that the U.S. government came to the rescue with a commitment to construct a new canal completely on U.S. territory. Hailed as one of the engineering marvels of the epoch, the All-American Canal since the early 1930s has been providing some 700 farmers in the Imperial and Coachella valleys with all the water they want. Rising urban demand for water has turned the heads of city planners in San Diego and Los Angeles toward the Imperial Valley, where much water is lost through wasteful irrigation practices and through immense seepage from the All-American Canal. It has been estimated that some 106,000 acre-feet of water would be saved per year if the canal were completely lined in concrete to prevent seepage.

But what seems an ideal solution—and one that adheres to conservationist principles—has touched off new cross-border tensions over water-resource sharing. On the Mexican side, groundwater users are protesting that the proposed, and congressionally approved, canal-lining project will mean economic ruin. The water that seeps through the sands below the All-American Canal is not lost but instead serves to recharge the aquifer. It is then pumped to the surface again through hundreds of wells located on the Mexican side.

So who really owns this water? The answer to that question will not come easily since there are good legal arguments proffered by both sides and because little is known about sources, quantity, and cross-border flow of aquifers.[30] But more than the complexity of water rights in this individual and unusual case, the controversy over the All-American Canal may finally force Mexico and the United States to address the pressing issue of shaping an international treaty that provides for the equitable and sustainable mining of transboundary aquifers. As it is, both sides are busily pumping as fast as they can to quench the thirsts of area farmers, industries, and cities.[31]

This pumping frenzy would be all right if the reserves, called *bolsones* in some areas, were being recharged as fast as they were being mined. But the reserves represent millions of years of rainfall and surface seepage. With an average annual rainfall of three inches in Mexicali-Calexico or even eight inches in El Paso-Juárez, combined with the extreme exploitation of surface waters in the borderlands, the recharge rate is extremely slow. The discharge of treated wastewaters into the groundwater basins can help build up groundwater reserves, but this does not come close to resolving the escalating crisis of diminishing groundwater supplies.

In the El Paso area, for every twenty gallons of water extracted each year from the Hueco Bolson only one gallon is restored. As a result, this reserve—which serves as the sole water source for Juárez and provides about two-thirds of El Paso's water—probably will be sucked dry of potable water in thirty years.[32] Since 1900, groundwater levels have dropped seventy-three feet in El Paso and eighty-five feet in Juárez—a rate of decline that has speeded up in recent years.[33]

An interesting twist on the Hueco Bolson drawdown saga is that both El Paso and Juárez, recognizing the dangerous implication of their mutual dependence on this one reserve, have cast their eyes west to the nearby Mesilla Bolson, another transboundary aquifer that lies almost exclusively under New Mexico. In negotiations and court cases with New Mexico, El Paso has failed to gain access to the Mesilla Bolson, although it did reach an out-of-court settlement with New Mexico that calls for water to be shipped from the Elephant Butte reservoir (created by a dam on the Rio Grande) by canal for El Paso's use. No U.S. court, however, can stop Juárez from pumping water out of the same contested aquifer, small amounts of which are now being appropriated to meet the water needs of Mexico border residents.

An international groundwater treaty or including groundwater concerns more explicitly within the purview of the IBWC are possible solutions.[34] More than twenty groundwater basins lie beneath the border. In most cases, the groundwater reserves exploited on one side of the border come from the same basins that the other side is also depleting. But what makes good sense makes bad politics. The four U.S. states touching Mexico are the country's largest groundwater users and vehemently reject proposals to share their reserves with other states, let alone Mexico.

All four states have different and conflicting laws regulating groundwater appropriation. In Texas the laws of the Wild West prevail, allowing the person with the bigger and faster pump to use as much water as is wanted—the result being disastrous drops in groundwater levels throughout the state.[35] Finally waking up to the fact that diminishing groundwater reserves are undermining the state's future economic and environmental stability, the Texas Water Commission in 1992 took the unusual step of declaring one aquifer that reaches into the borderlands an underground river; underground rivers, like surface waters, are subject to state control. New Mexico—where the strict rule of prior appropriation is regulated by the state—has the most enlightened and most tightly controlled groundwater pumping.[36] Although the rule of prior appropriation is more equitable than the "right to capture" principle that applies in Texas, it is not a doctrine that encourages water conservation or the use of water-saving technology; rather, it encourages the user to exploit as much groundwater as possible.[37] In Mexico the federal government regulates water rights in its determination of what constitutes the public good, but in practice water rights are a free-for-all in which the most powerful interests usually win, often with the direct support of the government.

For its part, the IBWC has generally stayed clear of groundwater issues. Except for some regulation of groundwater pumping in the Yuma-San Luis area, the binational commission has little authority over groundwater conflicts, except by way of offering technical consultation. In 1973 the groundwater issue was mentioned in one of the commission's amendments (or minutes). Minute 242 provided that "each nation shall consult prior to undertaking any new development of surface or groundwater in its own territory in the border area that might adversely affect the other country." In the same minute, the IBWC excused itself from any major role in groundwater conflicts "pending the conclusion by the governments of the United States and Mexico of a comprehensive agreement on groundwater in the border areas."[38] Although groundwater issues are discussed confidentially by the IBWC and its counterpart in Mexico, it has been unwilling to play a lead role in promoting the importance of apportioning groundwater resources along the border.

In fact, such a groundwater accord has not even been seriously discussed by the two nations. But the conflict over the rights of seepage from the All-American Canal may be what is needed to push such a treaty forward. As both nations see that the future of the borderlands is endangered by dramatic drops in the groundwater tables, support for a groundwater treaty may expand even among the U.S. border states. Meanwhile, the prevailing rule seems to be a race to the bottom of the aquifer. This lack of regulation and institutional controls fosters overdevelopment of the borderlands, paving the way for social and economic crisis while aggravating border tensions.[39]

Although most binational water conflicts have focused on the distribution and quality of Colorado River waters, the sharing of the Rio Grande has also been problematic.[40] Because of the tremendous population growth along the Rio Grande, the future of agricultural development in the lower Rio Grande Valley and other areas is threatened. Water-deficient cities like El Paso are buying water from water users in rural areas, converting irrigation water into drinking water. In the lower Rio Grande Valley—a region that depends on the river for 98 percent of its water needs—farmers use about 90 percent of the water. They could use more, too, since the valley has another 500,000 acres that could be farmed if irrigation water were available at a reasonable price.

But with the region's 4.3 percent annual rate of population growth driving up the cost of water, the agricultural economy is beginning to suffer. Water quality is also quickly deteriorating. Like the Colorado River, increasing salinity is making the water more difficult to treat and hazardous for crops. Farmers also contaminate the Rio Grande through the extensive runoff of pesticides, fertilizer, and herbicides that converts the Rio Grande into a chemical stew. The biggest culprit in the contamination of the Rio Grande, however, is probably the wastewater that is discharged into the river from both sides.

It is in the hundreds of *colonias* lining the Rio Grande that one can best appreciate the magnitude of population growth—and the accompanying water problems—along the Texas-Mexico border. Scattered behind the bluffs and mesas of the high Chihuahuan desert around El Paso are dozens of makeshift communities that lack water and sanitation facilities. Although historically El Paso has resisted popular pressure to extend city water to the *colonias*, it has not hesitated to resort to artful gerrymandering to annex undeveloped land slated for affluent suburbs. Responding to the complaints of *colonia* residents and their advocates, El Paso's former water district director in 1987 offered this advice: "All they have to do is boil it, or put a few drops of bleach in it or toss in some pills like we did in Europe during the war."[41] Since then the city has adopted a more enlightened attitude and has worked with citizens groups and the Texas Water Development Board to bring water to the *colonias.*

The water conflicts arising along the border—from the controversy over the lining of the All-American Canal to the demands of *colonia* residents for water services—are typical of a rapidly developing region with diminishing natural resources. Both sides of the border are short of water, and on both sides the competition for scarce water between rural and urban users is intensifying.

In the U.S. Southwest this conflict between agricultural and city users is aggravated by two additional factors: the increasing demands of upper basin states for their share of the surface water and the mounting demands of the Indian tribes seeking to secure their treaty and prior appropriation water rights. Because the upper basin states never fully appropriated their stipulated share of Colorado River water, the lower basin states, mainly California, have grown accustomed to using more water than was apportioned to them. But with the expanding water demands of the upper basin states and the coming on-line of the Central Arizona Project (meeting the needs of Tucson and Phoenix), the water supply future of Southern California looks increasingly grim.[42] San Diego, which imports 90 percent of its water, depends on the Colorado River for 70 percent of its total water needs. To meet the water demands of San Diego and Los Angeles, city and state planners will increasingly be looking at the cheap water enjoyed by agribusiness, which soaks up about 80 percent of California's water. Large and inefficient water users, such as the rice and livestock industries, will have a particularly difficult time justifying their appropriation of subsidized water in the desert environment of Southern California.

As the dimensions of the water crisis become clearer, the urgency for water conservation will become more apparent. Already cities across the borderlands, from El Paso to San Diego, are limiting lawn watering and car washing to certain times of day and days of the week. Especially in times of drought, lush green golf courses and swimming pools in desert hot spots like Palm Springs may be luxuries that California will no longer be able to afford. As they get the message that water is not an unlimited resource—and that it stands to become increasingly costly—farmers and ranchers are looking to conservation, installing more efficient drip irrigation systems to replace wasteful spraying.

The same scarcity and conservation issues face the Mexican side. Desert cities such as Juárez, Nogales, Mexicali, and Tijuana are exploding with hundreds of thousands of new residents demanding municipal water. These cities have fallen far behind in meeting these demands, but to expand their water services puts them in direct competition with the farm sector, which in Baja California uses more than 90 percent of the available water. With the growing demand for produce in the Mexican border cities and in the United States, agriculture could expand further, if only there were more water.

Not only are many of the water concerns on either side of the border similar, but they are in most cases closely linked. Take, for example, the case of the widespread lack of water and wastewater treatment facilities in Mexico, which is causing a public health crisis on both sides of the border. As a result, U.S. border cities are calling on the federal government to help solve the wastewater treatment problems of the Mexican border cities. One El Paso study predicted that without financial assistance "the area will become an example of everything that is wrong with free trade between countries that do not have equal economic status."[43] Clearly, there is also the urgent need for joint planning efforts. In the case of El Paso-Juárez, until 1991 there had not been any direct formal contact between the respective water utilities despite their using the same water and facing the nightmarish scenario of the wells running dry.[44] Mushrooming development throughout the borderlands threatens environmental disaster but also may contribute to border tensions. At least one high-ranking Mexican official who has followed U.S.-Mexico water issues closely predicts that by the year 2000 the United States will be unable to meet its commitments under the 1944 treaty.[45]

Badlands Biosphere

Concerns about diminishing water supplies point to a broader crisis threatening to turn the fragile border environment into a wasteland. Ironically, that is exactly how many outside the region have customarily viewed the borderlands—as wastelands without beauty or life. But many who have lived along the border see instead a land of enchanting panoramas, glorious sunsets, and endless diversity.

Until the late 1800s the borderlands were regarded as badlands or *malpaís*—the realm of rattlesnakes, *bandidos*, and desert rats. But when eastern doctors began prescribing the Southwest climate for treating pulmonary ailments, the environment in places such as Tucson, Phoenix, and Albuquerque came to be regarded as less hostile and more healthful. More recently the U.S. southern border became one of the homing spots for the millions of elderly snowbirds seeking warmer and cheaper climes in which to spend their retirement years. In contrast, Mexico's northern border region was never valued for its therapeutic properties. Nor it is a place where Mexico City residents dream of living their last years. Rather it has been the lure of border trade and services—and eventually maquila manufacturing—that has always shifted Mexican attention northward.

With the border's aridity comes an environmental fragility that is increasingly evident. The wide-open spaces of desert grama grass and sagebrush were turned over to cattle, both north and south of the border, and the result has been severe overgrazing and associated erosion. Over time stirrup-high grasslands became mesquite deserts, and arroyos cut their way deeper through the barren plains following heavy summer rains. Studies of the state of Sonora have pointed out that more than 70 percent of the land shows signs of severe erosion.[46] The process of desertification continues to turn some beautiful borderlands into what are truly badlands.

Despite its despoliation and rapid urbanization, the borderlands remain an enchanting and visually spectacular place.[47] In fact, the term *desertification* tends to underscore the common perception that deserts are unnatural and unappealing. "But a true desert can't be created," said Caroline Wilson, interpretive specialist for Organ Pipe Cactus National Monument in Arizona. "Deserts are no more manmade than are rain forests or prairies."[48]

Although the danger signals about the unsustainability of present development trends are already flashing, for the time being the region seems slated for more growth. Cities keep expanding, and the wells just get deeper. This uncontrolled and undirected growth is taking an increasing toll on the borderlands biosphere. Yuccas and cacti are being yanked out of the desert and transplanted to the front yards of water-conscious homeowners in El Paso, San Diego, and Tucson. One analyst at the College of Sonora in Hermosillo claimed that the Sonoran desert is being turned into a barren strip as a result of all the desert trees and plants being smuggled into the United States. Mexican researchers have revealed that many fish species in the Rio Grande have been lost or severely threatened because of increasing salinity, and that unregulated pumping has substantially decreased spring flow in the border states of Coahuila and Nuevo Leon.[49]

Water pollution is having a devastating impact on marine life at either end of the border. Clams and sand dollars, once abundant in the South Bay area below San Diego, are now rare. The dumping of sewage into the ocean has taken its toll on shellfish, crabs, and game fish. Environmentalists in Mexico warn that the Gulf of California is rapidly losing its ecological stability, as evidenced by the plummeting shrimp catches and the gradual disappearance of endangered species such as the vaquita porpoise and the totoaba fish, which tastes like white sea bass and often grows to six feet in length. Just as harmful as pollution to this rich marine ecology are the loosely regulated fishing industry and the sports fishermen from Southern California.[50]

In the Gulf of Mexico some 95 percent of the commercial fish and shellfish rely on coastal estuaries (wetlands and adjacent sea grass habitats in open water) during at least part of their life cycles. Oil production and coastal urbanization in both the United States and Mexico have resulted in serious water pollution, which has led to the permanent or conditional closure of 57 percent of the shellfish-growing areas along the U.S. Gulf Coast. Up to 3,000 square miles of bottom waters off the Louisiana and southeastern Texas coasts are known as dead zones where nothing lives because pollutants have depleted the oxygen. Other water pollution issues in the Gulf of Mexico include the escalating marine debris that poses a special threat to sea birds and marine mammals.[51] Texas Water Commissioner Gary Mauro testified at the EPA's 1992 hearings on its border environmental plan that the plan ignored the Gulf of Mexico, which he called the "most important border" between the two nations and the area that represents "our greatest risk of bilateral environmental calamity."

Rose Farmer of the National Audubon Society in Brownsville pointed out that the lower Rio Grande Valley is really a delta region: This means that all the liquid wastes in this expansive area eventually make their way to the Gulf of Mexico. Once characterized by extensive palm and bush forests, the region is now a mix of plowed farmland, trailer parks, and orchards where most of the native animal species are threatened or endangered. Environmentalists charge that the deformed birds and fish found in the Rio Grande and the Laguna Madre estuary on the Gulf of Mexico are the products of uncontrolled population and industrial growth in the region.[52] According to the Texas Land Commission, more than a third of the gulf shellfish beds are contaminated, and a 3,000-square-mile oxygen-deficient dead zone exists off the Texas and Louisiana coasts—at least partly created by increased U.S. and Mexican offshore petroleum development.[53]

Exotic Goods

As an international crossroads, the U.S.-Mexico border serves as a center of commerce in exotic species, especially birds. The U.S. Fish and Wildlife Service estimates that wildlife species with a retail value of $10 million to $50 million are smuggled into the United States each year from Mexico.[54] Like most smuggling businesses, the illegal trade in tropical birds and animals involves a broad range of operatives—from the big entrepreneur to the small-time contraband artist. Bill Myers, one of only four U.S. Fish and Wildlife Service inspectors along the border, said that illegal birds often come in with undocumented immigrants. "It's as constant as drugs," observed Myers.[55]

In Brownsville it is common to see Mexicans selling birds out of paper bags at the flea market. At shops near the Tijuana market you can buy green and yellow parrots prepared for a quiet border crossing, their beaks and wings taped and wrapped inside a paper bag small enough to stuff inside your jacket. Although Mexico prohibits the export of birds, roughly 150,000 exotic birds are smuggled into the United States each year—most of them through Mexico from Central and South America.[56] It is a high-profit, low-risk business, one that is fueled, like the narcotics trade, by the large U.S. demand. In many cases the trade is transacted in back rooms much like the stolen art business, but smugglers also sell exotic species openly to pet stores or through bird magazines with no questions asked.

The World Wildlife Fund, Defenders of Wildlife, and other conservation groups warn that the increased U.S.-Mexico trade that will result from a free trade accord will create opportunities for expanded trafficking in wildlife from the tropics.[57] The United States stations four U.S. Fish and Wildlife Service inspectors along the border but plans no increase in agents despite projected rises in trade. In 1991 Mexico signed the Convention on International Trade in Endangered Species (CITES) prohibiting commercial trade in endangered species, but enforcement is minimal. The country serves as an international trading center and pipeline for protected animals from all over the world, but particularly from Latin America. Mexican conservationists claim that the traffic in pelts of such endangered feline species as jaguars, ocelots, and pumas is contributing to the disappearance of these wildlife in Mexico.[58] The fondness of many U.S. tourists and consumers for boots and other leather goods fashioned from the skins of turtles, lizards, and caribou is also eliminating Mexican wildlife. Despite their complete protection under Mexican law, many endangered species, such as sea turtles and crocodiles, continue to be threatened by illegal trade with the United States. Wildlife trade along with the continued clearing of forest for timber, agriculture, and pasture has resulted in the complete loss of 50 percent of the country's forests and meant that only 25 percent of the remaining forests are fully biologically intact.[59]

Another dimension of illegal wildlife trade has been the movement northward of such desert and tropical plants as cacti and orchids. Generally these plants are not cultivated commercially in Mexico but are part of an unsustainable harvest and trade in wild specimens in Mexico. One such problem is the contraband trade in mesquite from the high deserts of northern Mexico. Enterprising importers are scouring the high deserts of northern Mexico to meet the rising U.S. demand for steaks flavored by mesquite charcoal. Urban development, ranching (including the introduction of especially destructive breeds of livestock), and the recent surge of fuel-wood cutting are stripping arid areas that suffer among the world's slowest rates of vegetation recovery. As the shrubs, trees, and cacti disappear, the ambient temperatures in some areas have increased by several degrees. According to Ciprés Villarreal, president of the Mexican Ecology Movement, the Sonoran desert is turning into a Sahara-like inferno because of rapid loss of vegetation.[60]

Perhaps it is because this arid land seems so endless that it is treated so carelessly by many of its inhabitants and visitors. But the natural environment of the U.S.-Mexico border region—its water, plants, animals, birds, and even insects—is seriously endangered. Biologists warn that hundreds of plants, including dozens with known benefits to humans, merit special conservation efforts.[61] Obviously, conserving the borderlands bioresources cannot be a one-sided initiative but will depend on binational efforts, including joint environmental regulation programs and the creation of an international park system along the border.

Chapter 2

The "Other America"

Environmental crisis along the U.S.-Mexico border is nothing new to most residents in the area. Over the past three decades they have seen their streams and rivers die, their air become clogged with pollution, and the natural habitats for wildlife disappear. Closely related to these assaults on shared ecosystems is a public health crisis characterized by high incidences of such infectious diseases as hepatitis and tuberculosis. Frightening new reports of birth deformities, possibly the result of parental exposure to toxic chemicals, have given the public health crisis a doomsday quality.

For many years Dr. Laurance Nickey, director of the El Paso City–County Health and Environment District, has been sounding the alarm. Born in El Paso, Nickey went swimming in the Rio Grande as a boy but now is afraid to go near the river for fear of all the disease and toxicity it channels. "The U.S.-Mexico border is burning, and the flames need to be extinguished before they consume us," warned Nickey. In his view, border communities like El Paso are "the other America, the forgotten America."[62]

Not all those living along the border feel as strongly about environmental health issues as Dr. Nickey, but in places such as El Paso, Matamoros, Nogales, and San Diego there is rapidly spreading concern about the degradation of the natural and human environments. San Diegans are most upset about the pollution of their beaches by untreated waste from booming Tijuana, while those living along the Rio Grande complain that the border river has turned into a sewage ditch. On the Mexican side, concern is growing about the health effects of all the toxic wastes being dumped by border industries.

It was not until the 1980s that environmental issues on the U.S.-Mexico border were given major diplomatic attention. Although concerns about water quality and sanitation had been raised as early as the 1940s, they were localized, low-level issues. However, it was the salinity crisis in the Colorado Basin—not water contamination—that resulted in the first serious diplomatic tensions between the two countries over water quality in the borderlands.[63] Gradually complaints about the transboundary flows of sewage and air pollution pushed the two governments to address border sanitation problems.[64] But not until the 1990 announcement of a proposed free trade agreement did the border environmental crisis become a full-blown foreign policy issue. Free trade suddenly pushed the "other America"—the one where Mexico and the United States meet—into the national spotlight.

Not all border residents are optimistic about the benefits of increased U.S.-Mexico economic integration—at least not from an environmental or public health perspective. With the increase of overland trade, cities such as Laredo and El Paso will have more trucks rumbling through their streets. But as one border city official remarked, economic development should mean more than becoming the nation's largest truck stop. For Jesús Reynoso, El Paso's air-quality supervisor, "Free trade will be an environmental disaster. More vehicles and more people mean more pollution."[65]

National environmental organizations, citizen watchdog groups, and the labor movement focused public and congressional attention on the borderlands in their attempt to forge a trade agreement that would adequately address health, safety, and environmental concerns. The border economy and society, while illustrative of the many benefits of close U.S.-Mexico relations, also reflect many of the problems resulting from U.S. trade and investment in Mexico. For opponents of a business-dominated free trade agreement, the borderlands present an excellent case study of the devastating health and environmental consequences of unregulated and undirected economic development.

Recognizing that environmental issues might become a sticking point in the effort to push a free trade accord through the U.S. Congress, the Bush and Salinas administrations quickly attempted to demonstrate their concern for the environmental and infrastructural crisis at the border. Previously the Mexican environmental agency SEDUE (later merged into SEDESOL) had concentrated what little regulatory capacity it had on the heavily polluted Mexico City metropolitan region. With the free trade debate stirring and U.S. concern about border pollution escalating, the Salinas administration opened new SEDUE/SEDESOL offices along the border and promised to deploy dozens of new agents. The flagship of this binational environmental campaign was the Integrated Border Environmental Plan (IBEP) coauthored by SEDUE and the EPA. Critics of the fast-track approach to free trade regarded the IBEP and other official environmental initiatives more as part of a lobbying blitz than as a demonstration of sincere concern and commitment. According to Mary Kelly, director of the Texas Center for Policy Studies, "In the rush to sign a free trade agreement, both the U.S. and Mexican governments are on the verge of relegating the border environmental issues to a high-profile sideshow, long on promises, but very short on meaningful changes and enforceable commitments to action." As Kelly noted, the IBEP did not even examine the potential environmental impacts of a free trade agreement on the border region.[66]

The new focus on the border, however, actually highlighted the fallacy of the free traders' standard argument that economic growth and a clean environment go hand in hand. Along the border, at least, that had certainly not been the case. The Border Industrialization Program of 1965 sparked a boom in population and economic growth, but in its wake came ecological catastrophe. Foreign investment and trade rose to unprecedented heights during the 1980s, but it was not until the free trade talks opened that the Mexican government demonstrated any serious concern for maintaining a clean border environment. On the U.S. side, communities watched as scores of Fortune 500 companies set up modern assembly plants in Mexico, but the borderlands seemed to look more like the third world all the time.

Attention to the border region has stirred up a heated debate about where financial responsibility lies. Who is to blame for the despoiled environment and for the public health crisis, and who should pay? For U.S. citizens living along the border, the answers come easily. Border communities—with the exception of San Diego—are among the poorest in the nation. Their tax bases do not even cover the cost of local public services, let alone extend to resolve international problems. Although many of the region's environmental problems, such as inadequate waste treatment facilities, come from the south side of the border, local government officials in the United States hesitate to blame Mexicans. Being from generally poor and crisis-ridden communities themselves, the officials are often sympathetic to the plight of Mexican border communities that do not have the financial resources to pay for needed environmental infrastructure projects. Nor is criticism of the maquila industry widespread on either side of the border, especially in official and business circles. The maquiladoras do boost the border economy—although not to the degree many would like—and there is a fear that too many regulations and taxes will drive away these footloose industries.

Instead, U.S. border communities look to Washington for assistance to solve what they believe are essentially international problems. But congressional representatives from the northern states ask why they should pay to treat sewage from Nuevo Laredo, to provide water services to the *colonias*, or to increase the public health budget of El Paso. These are essentially foreign aid projects, some members of Congress have contended, pointing out that the traditional manufacturing centers of the Northeast and Midwest are also suffering from economic hard times and deteriorating infrastructure.

This search by U.S. border communities for funds to solve environmental and public health crises is also laced with irony: Many of these same cities have for years been trying to sell themselves as havens from high taxes and wages. Cities like El Paso are still actively trying to entice businesses from other states to open maquiladoras in neighboring Juárez. Border communities are clearly right that they face problems of an international nature. Yet why should federal funds underwrite the solutions to environmental problems that have in part been created by U.S. companies that ran away to Mexico to escape higher wage rates and perhaps even environmental regulations at home?

In Mexico, while the government has agreed that it should pay for the pollution created on its side, it has other pressing concerns. Referring to the concern in San Diego that beaches have been closed because of inadequate or nonexistent sewage treatment in Tijuana, one government official commented, "You talk about the problems of surfers on Imperial Beach. Go to the neighborhoods in Tijuana where they have no pavement, no water or sewage system, and tell them about the big problem of the surfers."[67]

Black Waters

At the historic La Fonda Inn in Santa Fe, conference participants made their way past demonstrators to attend the First Annual U.S.-Mexico Border Environmental Assembly in June 1992. It was a conference sponsored by the Border Progress Foundation, a private, nonprofit organization founded with a seed grant from the EPA. But demonstrators from the Coalition for Justice in the Maquiladoras and even a few skeptics attending the assembly considered the gathering a sham. Instead of an honest effort to resolve border environmental problems, they saw the affair as part of a well-orchestrated public-relations effort to push through a free trade agreement.

The protestors thought that the conference participants, mostly government and industry officials, were due for a reality check. Wearing rubber gloves, one of the protestors presented the conferees with a jar of dark, fetid water drawn from one of the sewage canals that run behind the maquiladoras in Matamoros. Many of the local government officials from the borderlands also thought that the conference sponsors needed some shock treatment. "I've got some news for those from Washington, Mexico City, or Austin for that matter," offered El Paso county health supervisor Dr. Laurance Nickey. "Santa Fe may be a very nice place, but it is not a border town. Next time they want to talk about the border they should have their conference in a real border city like El Paso so they can really see the problems we face."[68]

Even a short visit to El Paso or Ciudad Juárez, or any of the other border twins, reveals the severity of the region's environmental crisis. It quickly becomes apparent that the international boundary is no barrier to pollution. Rising 828 feet next to the Rio Grande in El Paso is the smelter emissions stack of ASARCO, a transnational corporation long considered one of the nation's worst industrial polluters.[69] Recent pollution control and cleanup measures have significantly reduced arsenic and lead emissions, but the air and water pollution from the smelter and El Paso's large refineries continue to present a cross-border pollution concern. In the mornings, the Mexican *colonia* residents on the banks of the Rio Grande claim they can taste metal in the air.[70]

It is the same story throughout the borderlands. Environmental problems of one side sooner or later also become the problems of the opposite side. Eighty years of clouds of white dust containing smelter discharges and raw sewage that rises from Agua Prieta's unpaved roads have settled over Douglas, Arizona. Knowing that untreated wastes from Tijuana and its 530 maquilas flush into the Pacific Ocean keeps many San Diegans from chancing a dip into their coastal waters. Meanwhile, San Diego reciprocates by dumping its treated sewage waters into the Pacific Ocean off Point Loma. A steel fence erected to guard the U.S. border runs between Mexicali and Calexico, but its effectiveness is limited. The New River, reputed to be one of North America's most contaminated rivers, flows north past the Mexicali's maquiladoras and sewerless *colonias*, under the border fence, and into the Imperial Valley.

The transboundary dimensions of contamination reach beyond the air and water to food. Fruits and vegetables sold on the streets of U.S. border cities are cultivated using wastewaters for irrigation, and the produce is then often carried by hand across waterways like the Rio Grande that are highly contaminated with raw sewage. Both the Mexican vendors and their contraband produce carry strains of such infectious diseases as hepatitis, dysentery, and even cholera— just one reason why the disease statistics of many U.S. border towns remind one of third world health profiles.[71]

The border area, according to the American Medical Association, is "a virtual cesspool and breeding ground for infectious disease."[72] The main vehicle for disease transmission is what is called *aguas negras* (black water) throughout Latin America. *Aguas negras* is a generic term that describes most wastewater—the murky liquid that flows out of homes, neighborhoods, and industries in areas without sewers and wastewater treatment plants. As border cities expand so do the massive quantities of sewage. In the absence of industrial waste treatment facilities, mixed in with fecal matter are the chemical wastes from industrial manufacturers, mostly maquiladoras. Historically most Mexican towns have treated their *aquas negras* just as most individual families have: letting it flow off out of sight and out of mind. Finding more sanitary alternatives has usually not been a priority for either the poor Mexican family or the financially strapped municipal government. Nor have border industries in Mexico made proper waste disposal a priority. Extending electricity and water lines are the first development priorities. Although many Mexican border cities now have drainage systems in place, effective wastewater treatment is still a rarity.

Along the border the *aguas negras* have become so voluminous that they can no longer be ignored. Running eighteen miles along the edge of Juárez and only a couple hundred yards from the international border with El Paso is a large ditch (the *acequia madre*) that *juarenses* also call *El Agua Negra*. Every day this city of 1.2 million people produces some thirty million to sixty million gallons of untreated wastewater. The black water is pumped out of the city and into outlying agricultural areas or into the Rio Grande.

The absence of a waste treatment facility in Juárez is not the exception. Instead it reflects the state of sewage disposal along the length of the U.S.-Mexico border. Although Juárez and other border cities have begun building waste treatment plants, the heart of the problem is the tremendous and virtually unplanned population and industrial growth of the region. This growth, when combined with the generalized poverty of the borderlands and the lack of public financial resources, has made it difficult for government officials, particularly on the Mexican side, to maintain adequate sanitation and treatment facilities. In Mexico the absence of sewage systems is widespread and extensive—from the largest to the smallest population centers.

But the problem is not confined to south of the border. Hugging the border on the U.S. side are the hundreds of uncharted subdivisions called *colonias* that lack both water and sanitation systems, adding to the black water problem. Even when sewage treatment structures are in place in U.S. border cities, they often fail to meet federal standards and resort to the dubious practice of dumping treated water into nearby rivers and oceans. Both El Paso and Las Cruces, New Mexico, have been cited by state and federal authorities for dumping untreated sewage into the Rio Grande.[73]

Concern about the declining quality of the water on the border has exploded in recent years to become one of the main sources of cross-border tensions. But almost a half-century ago, when the two nations established the binational International Boundary and Water Commission, water pollution was not even a topic of discussion. The 1944 treaty that established the commission set up the legal context for the integrated management of all U.S.-Mexico water conflicts. Focusing mainly on the sharing of surface water, the IBWC paid relatively little attention to the crisis of water pollution until the late 1970s, when public outcry made it a hot international issue. In 1979 the IBWC specifically acknowledged its responsibility in resolving waste treatment problems with the promulgation of its Resolution of Sanitation Problems.[74] Even so, the commission has been slow to act, and environmentalists have frequently criticized it for narrowly construing the phrase *border sanitation problems* and limiting its concern to projects such as sewage disposal works.[75] So bad is the reputation of the IBWC among many border activists that many are convinced that the mandate for this binational organization should not be explicitly extended to all water-quality issues because it would do an unacceptable job.

Most transboundary water quality surveys indicating industrial pollution along the border have been undertaken by private groups, such as the Border Ecology Project or the National Toxic Waste Campaign, not by the IBWC—or the EPA or its Mexican counterpart SEDESOL. For its part, the IBWC has collected hydrological data on transboundary groundwater, but it has been unwilling to stick its neck out on this issue by releasing the results of its studies or proposing solutions to this developing crisis. Such inactivity and irresponsibility have led many to call for a radical revamping of the IBWC or for the creation of a more environmentally conscious binational commission.[76] For many environmentalists and local government authorities on the border, hope that the two federal governments would begin to devote more serious attention and financial resources to resolving the water-quality crisis was dashed in 1992 with the publication of the Integrated Border Environmental Plan. The plan met with sharp popular criticism because of its narrow scope, lack of funding guarantees, and vague promises.

The fouling of surface and groundwater occurs on both sides of the border and generally results from untreated or inadequately treated human and industrial wastes as well as from the increased salinity arising from the overuse of scarce water supplies. Along the U.S.-Mexico border, twin cities face increasingly severe water pollution. The ditches and rivers have a different odor, color, and character depending on their location. In some places the "water" is unusually bubbly, apparently because of rapid organic waste decomposition. Near industrial sites a rock thrown in a ditch will release ominous vapors from the darkness below. At other sites the odor of fecal matter is especially nauseating, while sometimes the smell has a more chemical bite. Usually the *aguas negras* are decked with a brownish froth, and one can often see the glint of unnatural colors. After dark the Tijuana River frequently turns a metallic red as the night lights mix with some unknown toxin. Squatter settlements are often found by the sides of these waterways, but evidence of other life is rare. In the few cases where water has been tested, fecal coliform counts are frightfully high. Mosquitoes also seem to thrive, and looking down into the New River in Mexicali, one can occasionally see a few fish—probably a mutant breed—cavorting in the waste stream.

At the border's western end the Tijuana River crosses the international line on its course toward the Pacific Ocean. Like most rivers and streams along the borderlands, it has turned into a sewage canal. Its putrid waters gurgle from decomposing waste, alarming area residents, who have formed a protest group called Citizens Revolting Against Pollution. The sewage coursing through the Tijuana River has threatened some of the most beautiful beaches in Southern California. Joggers still run along the beaches, and a few foolhardy surfers ignore the posted warnings: *Contaminated with Sewage. Keep Out. Avoid All Contact.* A survey of its San Diego members by the Surfrider Foundation detected such health problems as ear infections, hepatitis, giardia, and other gastrointestinal problems.[77]

Unlike some other Mexican border cities, Tijuana has its own waste treatment facilities. But these overloaded and inefficient plants do not have the capacity to process all the sewage and industrial wastes produced by this 1.7-million-person metropolis. At least a third of the city's liquid waste goes untreated, and much of that flows northward into San Diego County through the Tijuana River and assorted gullies and gulches. Various solutions have been proposed, but many people are skeptical that the problem will ever be solved. And there is also much disagreement about who should pay to treat Tijuana's wastes.

One answer has been simply to pipe the wastewaters back to Mexico in what is known as a "return to sender" solution. But it has been an exercise in futility, since Tijuana does not have the facilities to treat this waste. Furthermore, the wastes that are piped into waste treatment plants are inadequately treated and then flow back up along the coastline to sully San Diego beaches and coastal waters. Lately San Diego has been treating the ten million to thirteen million gallons of waste that flows through the Tijuana River at its own Point Loma Wastewater Treatment Plant.

All is not well on the U.S. side either. The EPA has a four-year-old lawsuit accusing the city of San Diego of endangering the environment and human health by inadequately treating its sewage. The Point Loma facility is overloaded, and its 2.2-mile drainpipe into the Pacific recently ruptured, spilling wastes onto city beaches. The best solution seems to be a $400 million treatment plant to be financed by a combination of city, state, and federal agencies along with a $50 million commitment from the Mexican government. But the unwillingness of many U.S. congressional representatives to fund border projects and of most border residents to pay for projects they consider a federal responsibility threatens completion of this and other environmental cleanup projects in the borderlands.

Even if the proposed wastewater treatment plant in the Tijuana River valley went forward, few would predict that the sewage problem in Tijuana-San Diego or any other twin city area would soon be solved. There would remain the problem of renegade waste that never enters the city's sewers because half the inhabitants are not hooked up to the municipal system. "One way or another, Mexico keeps growing and their sewage keeps coming over here," remarked David Gomez of Citizens Revolting Against Pollution.[78] Gomez and his group want San Diego to assume more responsibility for resolving the environmental health problems along the border. "If your moats are full of sewage," Gomez said, "it doesn't matter if you live in a castle."[79]

The U.S. border is so contaminated by untreated wastes from Tijuana that California health authorities have prohibited the sale of produce from the truck farms in the San Ysidro area. Along the entire length of the border prospective immigrants often wrap plastic bags around their feet and shins before crossing the rivers and waterways that mark the border. But keeping themselves dry is only one reason that they don the plastic wraps. At a place nicknamed Smugglers' Gulch on the Tijuana-San Diego border, one veteran immigrant explained that even with plastic coverings the sewage he had to wade through was so toxic that he often ended up with an itchy rash on his lower legs.[80]

For the immigrants, crossing the border into the United States often means wading across a border line of filthy water. And for health officials in San Diego and other border cities, that means exposing themselves and U.S. citizens to salmonella, shigella, cholera, and hepatitis. An increasing concern is that these *aguas negras* are laden with mosquito larvae, which are increasing the risk of outbreaks of even more exotic health threats such as malaria and encephalitis.

East of Tijuana lies Mexicali, the capital of Baja California, which has an elementary waste treatment facility unable to process all the city's wastes. Consequently, some of the city's raw sewage and industrial waste empties directly into the New River, which flows through Calexico, California, emptying eventually into the Salton Sea which lies southeast of Palm Springs. More than ninety toxic chemical compounds have been found in the New River, including carcinogens such as PCBs, trichloroethylene, acetone, and vinyl chloride. As in the San Diego area, residents of the Imperial Valley resent receiving Mexicali sewage. Some farmers complain that they are required to have their wastes treated before dumping them into the New River even though the river is already badly polluted with untreated sewage from Mexico.[81]

Since the late 1950s the Nogales border cities have had an international agreement whereby a waste treatment plant on the U.S. side would process the wastes from its twin city. The capacity of the treatment plant soon became overloaded by the wastes from the mushrooming population on the Mexican side. Another problem, and one that is common up and down the border, is that the sewer system in Nogales, Sonora, does not serve the majority of the city's residents. Instead, the liquid wastes accumulate in pungent pools and eventually trickle down the city's barren hills into arroyos often flowing across the border. As a result of all this raw sewage collecting in its streets, storm canals, and rivers, the hepatitis rate in Nogales, Arizona, is about twenty times the national average.

The Nogales Wash, which flows north from Mexico, regularly contains such toxins as mercury, nitrates, lead, and cyanide. So contaminated is this waterway that in 1991 it exploded, lighting a city block on fire in Nogales, Sonora. But the chemical pollution is not limited to surface transboundary flows. Water testing has revealed the existence of a ten-mile underground plume of chemical contamination flowing north into Arizona.[82]

Piperos are the salvation of hundreds of thousands of *colonia* residents on both sides of the border. These are the men who fill up tanker trucks with water for delivery to the dusty parts of town where water lines do not reach. Residents wait as the *piperos* pump a week's supply of water into fifty-five-gallon metal drums that once held industrial chemicals—the toxicity of which is often clearly (but in English) described on attached labels. But on the border one outrage always seems overshadowed by another. Such is the case in Nogales, Sonora, where the water the *piperos* deliver to the parched communities and to maquilas is itself badly contaminated by toxic chemicals. In spite of the existence of an alternative well, the city permits the *piperos* to continue to draw their water from a municipal well that was recently found to be polluted with industrial solvents. The Nogales Wash, which runs through town and near the polluted well, has been posted with *Danger, Keep Out, Polluted Water* signs on the U.S. side.[83]

Farther east, such cities as Nuevo Laredo that have no treatment facilities simply pump their wastes into the Rio Grande. As the river flows through downtown Nuevo Laredo, it has a fecal contamination level exceeding 200,000 coliform bacteria per milliliter—a thousand times the limit in Texas, which closes public recreation lakes if they have more than 200 bacteria per milliliter.[84] "It's like living in Calcutta," remarked Laredo resident Adolph Kahn, who is spearheading an effort to cleanse the Rio Grande.[85] Cities on the U.S. side such as Laredo and Brownsville also dump their wastewater in the river but only after a dual treatment and disinfection process.

Urbanization is the most obvious cause of the current water pollution crisis in the borderlands. Closely related to the uncontrolled population growth has been the industrial explosion over the past three decades, but particularly since the early 1980s. Just as the *juarenses* or the *tijuanenses* have no waste facilities, neither do most maquiladoras. Their liquid wastes, like those of the squatter colonies surrounding the factories, flow into ponds and ditches that eventually contaminate the rivers and groundwater. Toxic chemicals such as methylene chloride and toluene mix with human feces in the *aguas negras* of the U.S.-Mexico border. Yet another largely unaddressed sanitation problem along the border—and throughout Mexico—is the use of untreated wastewater to irrigate crops on the outskirts of urban areas. This practice represents a health threat not only to Mexican consumers but also to U.S. shoppers who buy fruits, vegetables, and meat produced in Mexico.

Darkened Skies

The uncontrolled flow of black waters may be the most serious environmental danger in the borderlands, but the darkening of the borderlands skies is probably the best evidence that borders do nothing to obstruct the free flow of pollution.

Many border towns have become large cities with freeways and skyscrapers, but the gritty dust of the border is still part of the picture. In fact, the skies over the borderlands are browner and dustier than ever. But what one sees, breathes, and smells in the air is not all dust. The winds now also carry alarming quantities of such pollutants as ozone, carbon monoxide, sulfur dioxide, and lead as well as particulate matter. Like the black waters of the border region, the brown pallor of these southwestern skies has become a major health hazard.

The full extent of air pollution along the border is not known. In major U.S. border cities, air monitoring stations do measure local pollution for violations of the U.S. National Ambient Air Quality Standards. Less is known about more remote locations on the U.S. side. But until recently there was no attempt to monitor air standards on the Mexican side. The Mexican government has promised to begin air pollution sampling, but as yet the full scope of the problem can only be guessed.

Vehicle emissions, dust from unpaved roads, and industrial pollutants are the major culprits. Carbon monoxide and ozone contamination is most serious in El Paso and San Diego because of the large size of these cities and the temperature inversions that afflict them. Increasingly many observers are directing blame at U.S. customs and immigrations officials whose slow border inspections keep incoming traffic backed up with engines running. So lethal are the resulting fumes that the customs officials are rotated every half-hour at some border crossings to give the agents some relief.

Lax vehicle emissions regulations in Mexico also contribute to high ozone and carbon monoxide levels across the border. It was not until 1991 that Mexico mandated that all new cars produced for the domestic market have pollution control devices. Because of the difficulty of finding unleaded gasoline in Mexico, there is a booming business among mechanics to remove the catalytic converters from cars imported from the United States. Border cities have recently begun enforcing emissions levels on newly registered cars. While applauding these new controls, health officials in El Paso point out that the maximum levels permitted in Juárez are 3.5 times higher than those enforced on the U.S. side. Another problem is the relative ages of cars on either side of the border. El Paso has more vehicles than Juárez, but the average age of those on the Mexican side of the border is almost twice that found on the U.S. side. In Juárez the average age of vehicles is twelve years.[86] As a result, the Mexican vehicles are far more likely to lack pollution control devices and to be poorly tuned.[87] Not only are Mexican vehicles generally older and poorly maintained, but they also use low-quality gasoline. On the U.S. side, regular gasoline has 0.1 grams of lead per gallon and unleaded contains just 0.05 grams, but in Mexico regular Pemex gas is loaded with 1 to 2 grams of lead, and unleaded gas also has a higher lead content. In Juárez an estimated 90 percent of the gas sold is leaded—in contrast with 15 percent across the border.[88]

A closely related problem is the flow of Mexican traffic into the United States. According to San Diego County Supervisor Brian Bilbray, vehicles coming from Mexico account for less than 1 percent of the city's traffic but produce 13 percent of the vehicle-generated pollution.[89] One solution would be to require Mexican vehicles to meet local standards for travel in the United States. But as with other attempts to control pollution along the border, proposals to enforce strict emissions standards mean additional economic hardships for a poverty-stricken population. As an environmental consultant observed, "To buy a set of points and plugs is a week's wage in Mexico. You can't expect them to spend a week's wages to meet our standards."[90]

In an attempt to meet federal air-quality standards, El Paso has recently begun to pave most of its dirt alleys and roads. But one has only to look across the Rio Grande at the dusty *colonias* on the Juárez hillsides to see that the high particulate concentrations in the city's air are not likely to improve appreciably even though some Mexican border towns have begun paving more of their roads.

The scene is repeated along the entire length of the border. The central portions of the Mexican border towns generally have paved streets, but outside the downtown areas extends an uncharted maze of dusty roads. Barren hillsides are covered with concrete and plywood shacks, and ankle-deep dust covers many of the streets during the dry seasons.

Actually, the longest-running concern about air pollution in the borderlands has not been about either carbon monoxide or particulate matter but rather about smelter pollution. Following a ground swell of citizen protests, the Mexican and U.S. governments undertook cooperative efforts to lower sulfur dioxide emissions from the copper-smelting operations on both sides of the Sonora-Arizona line involving smelters in Cananea, Nacozari, and Douglas (which was later shut down). Although greatly reduced, the emission of sulfur dioxide and trace minerals remains an environmental concern along this part of the border. Recent privatizations of Mexican mines, followed by the 1992 smelter reconstruction at Cananea, raise new concerns that the specific provisions of the 1983 binational agreement regarding smelter emissions from the Nacozari and Cananea smelters may not be respected.[91] Farther east in El Paso, the ASARCO copper smelter and the city's petroleum refineries also present a cross-border pollution problem.

Whereas the smoke belching out of ASARCO's smelter has diminished in recent years as the result of new pollution controls mandated by the government, citizen concern on both sides of the border has increasingly focused on other border industries, particularly the chemical factories and maquiladoras scattered along the Mexican side from Matamoros to Mexicali. In the Matamoros-Reynosa area alone, there have been seven major industrial accidents since the late 1980s that have sent more than 350 people to hospitals and forced thousands to flee their homes to avoid massive discharges of toxic fumes from chemical plants.

The most striking air pollution problem along the border is neither vehicle nor industrial emissions but the open fires on the Mexican side. Looking down on Juárez from the hills of El Paso, one can see wisps of gray smoke from household heating fires rising everywhere during the winter months. Darkening the skyline are the black plumes that result from the open burning of garbage at the city dump. A steady stream of smoke also rises from the part of town where brickmakers use old tires and sawdust to fire their kilns.

In Juárez, as in many Mexican towns, small industries and individual families generate heat during the winter months by making their own fires because they have no electricity or heaters. They burn wood, old tires, cardboard, and just about any kind of trash to fuel those fires—and the resultant smoke darkens the skies and clogs lungs on both sides of the border.

Considering the widespread poverty in Mexican border towns, it would be difficult for Mexican authorities to prohibit household fires that provide the only source of heat for many families. But the open burning of wastes in municipal dumps and the practice of burning old tires by brickmakers are problems that may be controlled more easily, as seen in Juárez where brickyards are being converted to gas-fired kilns. Still, the pervasive poverty in Mexico—not only of individual families but also of government institutions—stands as a major obstacle in the battle against pollution and for improved environmental health. As Jesús Reynoso, El Paso's air-quality supervisor, pointed out, "I don't even think Juárez owns a street sweeper."[92] Although generally an urban problem, air pollution is also a product of the rural borderlands. Tilled fields on both sides of the line and the common practice of burning ditch banks and fields further degrade the air.

Although primarily an environmental health issue, air pollution is also an aesthetic concern. The once deep-blue skies of the borderlands are losing their clarity. No longer an isolated and largely untouched region, the borderlands now share the environmental problems of other industrial and population centers.

Worsening air and water pollution add up to an alarming state of environmental health along the border. Texans living near the Rio Grande are three to five times more likely than other Texas residents to suffer from intestinal illnesses. In the border community of San Elizario, near El Paso, 90 percent of all adults contract hepatitis by age thirty-five, and there are more cases of tuberculosis in El Paso County than are found in nineteen states.[93] The incidence of most communicable diseases, including syphilis, is significantly higher in U.S. border communities than in the rest of the country.[94] In the poor *colonias* strung along the U.S. border, residents suffer third world rates of dysentery.

Disease, like air and water pollution, does not respect national boundaries. "We can't keep chicken pox north of the border and measles south," said one border health official.[95] To protect the health of their own citizens, U.S. border health authorities recognize the urgent need for increased cooperation with the Mexican government and nongovernmental organizations in matters of public health. This was brought home to many on the U.S. side by the spread of cholera in Mexico and then in April 1992 by the appearance of the first cholera case in Brownsville, Texas.

Although environmental health conditions are severe on both sides of the border, the problems are much worse on the Mexican side. Ironically, however, the health status along Mexico's northern border compares favorably with the nation as a whole. Although many of the environmental risk factors are similar, such as poor water and air quality, and inadequate health facilities, Mexican border residents are better off with respect to disease and mortality rates. This reduced health risk is apparently due to the relatively higher standard of living found in the northern borderlands.[96]

Border health officials in the United States feel overwhelmed by the spreading public health crisis throughout the borderlands. Cutbacks in federal and state health programs are largely responsible, but also worrisome has been the mushrooming of *colonias* on the U.S. side of the international line. The Mexican-American families who live in these isolated *colonias* usually dig their own wells, and they are often sunk fewer than ten yards from the outdoor privies they have constructed. In light of conditions such as these, the high incidence of communicable diseases—particularly gastrointestinal ailments—does not surprise public health officials in places like El Paso or Brownsville.

The public health crisis is magnified across the border, where rather than the exception the lack of adequate water and sanitation services is the rule. Also in stark contrast are the public health infrastructures in Mexico and the United States. The disparities are immense and expanding. The El Paso City–County Health and Environmental District, serving more than 600,000 people, operates on an annual budget of $11.3 million, while the 1.5 million population of Juárez is served by a health department with an estimated annual budget of just $500,000.

For residents of the borderlands, the public health crisis is not news. But as free trade talks heated up, horror stories about living and working in the border area made U.S. national headlines for the first time. City, county, and state officials in the United States took advantage of the rising national interest in the U.S.-Mexico border to alert the U.S. public and Congress to the third world conditions along extensive stretches of the border—and to ask for increased federal assistance. At the same time, activists questioning the advisability of a free trade treaty with Mexico and journalists examining U.S. trade and investment in Mexico highlighted the environmental and occupational health hazards associated with the maquila industry.

Maquiladoras suddenly found themselves under scrutiny not only for waste disposal practices but also for their treatment of their low-paid work forces. Environmentalists in the United States, thrust into the free-trade debate, began to express concern not only about natural resource issues but also about broader environmental health issues, such as the chemical pollution inside the maquiladoras and the unhealthy living conditions of maquila workers. For more than a quarter-century the maquiladoras had operated in relative obscurity. The Mexican government left the industry alone, imposing virtually no environmental regulations and giving the plants nearly free rein in their treatment of the work force.

Especially when compared with most local industries, the maquilas seem modern and attractive. Inside, many of these assembly plants have a high-tech ambience and are generally cool, clean, and bright—not your typical sweatshop. Although the maquiladoras may in fact have better and safer working environments than many Mexican-owned manufacturing plants, they have fallen far short of being responsible corporate citizens. Since 1965, when the maquiladora program was instituted, the maquilas have taken full advantage of Mexico's lax regulatory climate and the lack of unions. Assembly operations were transferred from the United States, but the environmental and occupational health standards were left at home. The results of this quarter-century of neglect are predictable: low occupational safety standards, contaminated water near the industrial parks, widespread illegal dumping, and little monitoring of the use and disposal of hazardous chemicals.[97] The foul-smelling liquid that the Coalition for Justice in the Maquiladoras presented to EPA officials in Santa Fe was offered as a symbol of all these abuses.

"The land will never be the same. It's lost," said Ernestina Sánchez, whose home sits next to the holding pond of Retzloff Chemical, a pesticides manufacturer in Matamoros. Her father established this neighborhood a half-century ago and her family used to be able to drink the well water here until the U.S. factories moved in.[98] Now the neighborhood smells as if it has just been sprayed with pesticides, and the groundwater is tainted by un-known substances.

Dipped into a chemical bath, the borderlands and its residents are learning just how hazardous some of the toxic chemicals that border industries use really are. One of the most shocking cases is that of the Mallory children—the daughters and sons of women who worked at the Mallory Capacitors plant in Matamoros during the 1970s. Doctors have identified at least fifty-four profoundly handicapped or deformed children—known in Matamoros as *los niños de Mallory*—born of mothers who worked at the plant. As part of their job, the Mallory workers washed capacitors in a chemical wash they called *Electrolito* 95, apparently containing polychlori-nated biphenyls (PCBs). The chemical would cover their hands and arms and sometimes splashed into their faces. The former maquiladora workers also say they suffered from rashes, head-aches, nausea, and fainting while employed at Mallory.[99]

The women are suing the company. But they may have diffi-culty in proving the link between their jobs and the fate of their children because tests have found no PCBs in either the mothers' or the children's blood. Another obstacle is getting the corporate father of the Mallory children to admit responsibility for the sins of a past owner. Ownership of the company has changed hands several times, from Mallory to Kraft to North American Capacitor Company to Black & Decker.

In 1991 the Brownsville area was hit by another disturbingly high cluster of deformed children. Doctors found thirty-one babies with neural tube defects in a twenty-five-month period—significantly higher than U.S. national or statewide rates for these birth deform-ities known as anencephaly. Since 1986 there have been more than eighty incidents of anencephalic babies in the lower Rio Grande Val-ley. Most were born within a couple of miles of the Rio Grande, and there was widespread speculation that the prevailing winds carried toxic chemicals discharged from Matamoros maquiladoras across the river into Brownsville. Others suspect that pesticides sprayed on nearby farms may be the culprit. A year-long study by the Centers for Disease Control and the Texas Department of Health was unable, however, to point to an environmental explanation for this abnormally high incidence of anencephalic babies. It did mention the environment, along with genetics, poor prenatal care, and malnutrition, as possible contributing factors. Mexico has one of the highest rates of anencephaly in the world—six times the U.S. rate and three times the rate for South America.[100]

The Coalition for Justice in the Maquiladoras blames the maquila industry, pointing to studies linking the use of two industrial solvents—xylene and toluene—to neural stem defects.[101] According to this activist group, at the time the anencephalic babies were conceived the Stepan Chemical Company and General Motors were dumping xylene and other hazardous chemicals into open canals behind their plants at levels that exceeded U.S. standards by 6,000 to 53,000 times. No firm link, however, has yet been established between the hazardous chemicals released by the maquiladoras and the large anencephaly cluster in this border city. One doctor in Brownsville speculated that this frightening deformity may actually be the "tip of the iceberg" of toxic chemical problems in the area, an observation that seemed to be confirmed by more recent revelations about high clusters of lupus in some border towns.[102] In reaction to the controversy, the Mexican government's secretary of health in Juárez issued a "Protocol for the Study of Anencephaly," which had the bad taste to advise that "with a free trade treaty imminent, it's essential to dispel doubts over Mexico's capacity to handle industrial wastes properly and the adequacy of its sanitation infrastructure."[103]

Assigning Blame

Traveling along the border one soon discovers that assigning blame for the environmental crisis is an exercise in futility. Who is the culprit? The Mexican government for not enforcing strict environmental controls, or the U.S.-owned maquiladoras that set lower environmental and occupational health standards than at plants based in the United States? Or is it really a cultural issue, or perhaps a problem rooted in the different levels of economic development found on either side of the border?

Even when responsibility can be fairly assigned, finger pointing does not help solve what usually have become common problems. Instead border communities and their government representatives increasingly realize that the time has come to search for common solutions to the mounting ecological catastrophe. Archie Close, El Paso regional director of the Texas Air Quality Board, expressed the common sentiment of border officials that "the problems are obvious, and so it serves no purpose to find fault with the other side because we need their cooperation to accomplish anything."[104]

Local authorities in the United States complain that federal officials fail to recognize the international causes of air-quality violations, and that regional offices of the EPA are ill-equipped to deal with binational issues.[105] Rather than waiting around for the federal governments to act, many border cities have initiated joint programs. El Paso, for example, regularly sprays the sewage canal in Juárez to suppress the mosquito population, and Douglas, Arizona, has offered to provide Agua Prieta with the pitch and slag to pave its dusty roads. The international border, however, places a severe limit on locally arranged solutions. Expressing this frustration, one San Diego official remarked, "We share the same air basin and the same sources of water for most things in Tijuana, but we sometimes have to wait for Washington to take the circuitous route to talk with Mexico City."[106] The fragmentation between various local, state, and federal agencies in the United States continues to obstruct solutions to the border's environmental crisis.

Yet even with better and quicker cross-border communications both on a local and national level, the problem of money remains. As Sergio Reyes Lujan, the former director of SEDUE and now the director of SEDESOL's National Institute of Ecology (INE), observed, "Everyone knows how to stop pollution in the river—you construct a treatment plant for the sewage. The technological solution is simple, but for economic reasons, many cities are not able to apply the solution."[107] But money is only part of the solution. Also lacking in Mexico are representative governments and legal systems in which local citizens can exert pressure on their government officials. In the United States, the mechanisms for citizen participation do exist but the voices of border residents are often ignored. Some also question the technology fix proposed by SEDESOL and the EPA, pointing out that more front-end solutions are needed to prevent hazardous wastes from entering the waste stream in the first place and to encourage more appropriate and natural solutions that contribute to sustainable development. Another concern is that increased attention to environmental problems in the borderlands may come at the expense of other region's in Mexico where environmental problems are at least as severe.

Local officials in U.S. border cities have applauded the promise of the Mexican government to increase SEDESOL's presence along the border but are waiting to see if it is more than a rhetorical commitment. Despite pronouncements that enforcement of environmental regulations would be dramatically increased, SEDESOL appears to be falling short on its promises. At the same time, border officials complain about the EPA's lack of presence along the border, despite all the rhetoric from Washington about its concern for border environmental problems. "The United States spends millions to help faraway countries," said Dr. Nickey. "Why can't we help the people who live next to us? By helping them, we help ourselves." Patrick Zurick, Nickey's counterpart in Nogales, Arizona, noted that the environmental and public health crisis along the border is not a local problem, but an international one. He complained, "It's as if we're supposed to be waiting for a body count before we get action."[108]

Chapter 3

The Poison Trail

International commerce and investment involve more than the cross-border flow of materials and money. Increasingly poisons also flow back and forth across borders. Because of stricter dumping laws in the United States and other developed nations, many firms are shipping their toxic wastes—legally or illegally—to third world countries where the regulatory climate is much looser.

Some corporations go a step farther. Frustrated by environmental health and occupational safety regulations, they pack up their plants—or at least the most hazardous operations—and move overseas, or south of the border. They run away to what some economists call "pollution havens." In these less regulated locations they can dump toxic chemicals and ignore standard occupational safety standards without any government agency looking over their shoulders.

In a global economy it is hard to have toxic chemicals and substances stay put. They sometimes boomerang across borders. This is especially true with contaminated food products, which may be sprayed with pesticides banned in the United States or irrigated with untreated wastewater, but which end up in the food baskets of U.S. consumers. Similarly, pharmaceuticals and various consumer products that have been either banned or restricted or are unregistered in their countries of origin often are exported to third world countries. This practice has been called the "corporate crime of the century."[109]

Neither do ecosystems respect international borders. Wildlife, such as birds found in the estuaries of the Gulf of Mexico and Southern California, have been found to have high levels of DDT in their tissue. Banned in the United States, DDT is used by the Mexican government for pest control. In the 1980s two environmental concerns—stratospheric ozone depletion and climate change due to the accumulation of "greenhouse gases"—gave environmentalism a new global context. Public concern and new scientific findings have combined to create a deepening sense of global interconnection. Not only are nations interconnected as contamination—in the form of acid precipitation, air pollution, marine and water pollution, and transboundary waste shipments—crosses national boundaries, but government officials and activists alike are finding that economic and environmental issues are also linked. No longer can such matters as trade, debt, or even personal lifestyle choices be separated from the environment.[110]

Circle of Poison Becomes Two-way Street

Free trade talk has renewed the circle of poison issue in the United States.[111] Environmentalists and consumer advocates are now warning that food-safety regulations protecting consumers against pesticide-tainted produce may be weakened as trade barriers break down. The fear is that pesticide residue standards will be harmonized downward so as not to act as a barrier to international trade. Another concern is that the threat of plant closures and relocation abroad will be used by industry to keep local and federal governments from imposing stricter environmental and safety standards for products and production.

In 1962 Rachel Carson's book *Silent Spring* alerted U.S. consumers to the frightening repercussions of uncontrolled agrochemical use on the natural and human environment. Gradually, stiffer food safety regulations were set by the EPA. Numerous pesticides, particularly the long-lasting organochlorines like DDT, were banned or heavily restricted in the early 1970s because they persist in the environment and accumulate in animal and plant tissue. Companies producing those and other chemicals began exporting them to countries like Mexico, where regulations were more lax or nonexistent.[112]

At the same time, the United States began importing more of its food, especially fruits and vegetables, from foreign countries. This set off fears of a circle of poison in which U.S. consumers were eating tomatoes, bananas, strawberries, and bell peppers contaminated by pesticides outlawed by the U.S. government but produced by U.S. companies and shipped abroad. To protect consumers and to allay fears about this circle of poison, the Food and

Drug Administration (FDA) placed agents along the border to inspect incoming produce.

With about three billion pounds of produce annually crossing the border from Mexico, finding pesticides on a strawberry or a head of lettuce can be a daunting task. A stream of refrigerated truckloads passes through customs from Mexico, supplying about half of the vegetables and fruits consumed in the United States during the winter months. Nationally, about 1 percent of imports are checked for illegal pesticide residues.[113] In contrast with the occasional character of food safety testing, most produce coming from Mexico is checked to guarantee that it is up to the cosmetic quality demanded by the U.S. market and to ensure that it does not carry insects that could menace U.S. growers.

Jack Grady, one of two FDA agents stationed at the El Paso border crossing, acknowledged that contaminated produce is not being stopped at the boundary. For one thing, he said, the FDA office is only open during weekdays while some truckers pass through customs on weekends or after 5:00 p.m. Moreover, the U.S. Department of Agriculture, which has to stamp all food shipments but which does not check for pesticides, commonly does not even notify the FDA that produce is at the dock. When Grady does take a sample, he ships it by bus to Dallas for a multiresidue laboratory test, and if the laboratory does not report back to him by 5:00 p.m. the next day the produce is free to enter the United States. FDA records in El Paso showed that some produce is, however, being stopped at the border—including recent shipments of lettuce, papaya, and squash, some of which were tainted with DDT.[114]

Of those Mexican vegetables and fruits that are tested, some tests have shown that pesticide residues are generally twice the levels commonly found on domestically grown produce, although only a small percentage is so high that the EPA considers it a threat to health.[115] About 5 percent of the tests reveal unacceptable residues—approximately double the rate for domestic samplings—but most of this contaminated produce is already purchased and consumed by the time the test results are available.[116] Of additional concern to those persnickety eaters who worry about the carcinogenic and gene-damaging properties of pesticides is the inadequacy of the FDA tests, which are capable of detecting fewer than half the estimated 600 pesticides on the market. According to Jay Feldman of the National Coalition

Against the Misuse of Pesticides, "The basic information that the EPA needs to make food-safety decisions does not exist for many widely used pesticides."[117]

As the U.S. border opens up to increased agricultural trade, the circle of poison issue has gained new attention. Like other environmental concerns, questions of pesticide use and abuse have suddenly become subjects of the international trade debate. Not just environmentalists and consumer advocates are grumbling about lax pesticide controls in Mexico. Agribusiness representatives like William Ramsey of the Western Growers Association have gone to Congress to complain that Mexican farmers enjoy an unfair advantage since "U.S. producers are unable to use some chemical tools that their counterparts in Mexico can utilize."[118]

As with other environmental issues, the problem in Mexico is not so much the absence of laws regulating pesticide use as the lack of enforcement. Pesticides that the government prohibits or restricts are commonly used, especially for the domestic market. Another concern is the lack of education about chemical inputs in agriculture. With the cutbacks resulting from structural adjustment measures in recent years, the Agriculture Ministry's extension department has all but disappeared. Mexican consumers are unprotected from high pesticide residues on produce—more and more of which is imported as trade barriers among the United States, Central America, and Mexico break down.

With an increasing percentage of the produce consumed in the United States coming from Mexico, there is obvious reason for concern—in terms of both food safety and economic competition. Five of the dozen agricultural chemicals labeled the "Dirty Dozen" by the Pesticide Action Network International are registered for restricted use in Mexico. These are chlordane, aldicarb, lindane, paraquat, and pentachlorophenol. Mexico growers also use thirty-six chemicals that are prohibited in many industrial countries or are found among the United Nations' list of extremely hazardous agrochemicals.

In Mexico there is extensive use of pesticides that are either banned or heavily restricted by the EPA. For example, the herbicide Haloxifop and the insecticide Protiophos are not registered in the United States because of their dangerous properties but are exported to Mexico. In fact, the Mexican government through its Fertimex state enterprise has long been the chief manufacturer of several of the organochlorine poisons, including DDT.[119] In 1992 the Fertimex division producing pesticides was privatized. It is now owned by an affiliate of Velsicol USA, which plans to continue production of DDT, BHC, parathion, and other dangerous pesticides.

It is also true that U.S. firms, prohibited from selling certain chemicals at home, either sell them to Mexico or have affiliates in Mexico processing and distributing EPA-restricted agrochemicals. Among the transnational corporations manufacturing pesticides in Mexico are such companies as Ciba-Geigy, Bayer, Du Pont, Dow Chemical, ICI, and Monsanto. About 30 percent of the pesticide compounds for which the EPA has not set residue standards (mostly because of their hazardous qualities) are registered for use in Mexico.[120] Pesticide companies in the United States export not only hazardous chemicals but also production technologies and facilities (which are often obsolete) to Mexico and other third world nations.[121]

To focus on the circle of poison issue, however, overlooks the other hazards of increased pesticide use. In Mexico pesticide use more than doubled in the 1980s, and the pesticides of choice have been mostly ones with EPA-established residue levels. As in the United States and other industrial countries, growers in Mexico— particularly vegetable and fruit producers—have largely desisted from using persistent organochlorines and have adopted less persistent organophosphates, which were discovered by scientists in their search to develop nerve gas.

But even though organophosphates are less persistent in the environment and in foods, they are actually far more toxic than the pesticides they have replaced. Parathion, for example, which is now commonly used in Mexico, is twenty to fifty times as toxic as DDT if taken orally or absorbed through the skin. The great advantage is that the organophosphates break down rapidly so that residues are minimal by the time the treated produce reaches the market or the laboratories for testing. According to one close observer of pesticide practices in Mexico, Angus Wright of California State University in Sacramento, it has become increasingly rare for Mexican agroexporters to use chemicals banned or heavily restricted in the United States. However, because of the acute toxicity of the organophosphates and other chemicals, such as the herbicide paraquat, that are now used, "the shift to EPA-approved chemicals has substantially increased the immediate public health danger."[122]

The circle of poison is still a concern, but the more critical health and safety issue in the vegetable and fruit industry is the welfare of the farmworkers who are directly exposed to these highly toxic agrochemicals. The tomatoes and strawberries that U.S. consumers now eat come largely from estates in the northwestern states of Baja California, Sinaloa, and Sonora, where Mixtec and Zapotec Indians work in a chemical fog. What U.S. consumers do not see or think about as they eat their blemish-free fruits and vegetables are the thousands of farmworkers poisoned each year by this intensive spraying.

Noting that area growers place little value on the lives of their destitute work force, a doctor in Hermosillo, Sonora, reported a dramatic rise in pesticide poisoning: "Farmworkers are expendable—and when they die it is just another dead Indian." He told of a case only a few days before an interview in which a young farmworker, Juan Zavala, died from poisoning by a synthetic fertilizer that is banned in the United States. On the same day at the same clinic where the farmworker died, three other farmworkers, ages fourteen, sixteen, and eighteen, were treated for burns, wounds, and inflammations caused by farm chemicals.[123] Each of the government's four Social Security clinics in the Culiacán Valley in Sinaloa reports from eight to ten cases of organophosphate poisoning a day during the winter months.[124]

Agribusiness throughout northwestern Mexico produces cosmetic fruits and vegetables for U.S. tables through a combination of chemical wizardry, heavy irrigation, and careful hand picking by low-paid workers. Women and men laborers are paid less than $5 for a ten-hour day, with the more ambitious or foolhardy—usually young men—getting a dollar or two more for pesticide duty. In the San Quintín Valley, south of Ensenada in Baja California, Mixtec Indian boys and men apply the chemicals to the strawberries, tomatoes, and cucumbers destined for the U.S. market. As they loaded up their backpack applicators before heading out to the fields on a summer morning, they explained that they grew accustomed to the bitter chemical smell of the pesticides even as they gasped for breath. Some complained of headaches and dizziness but generally thought that their youth and the kerchiefs worn as masks would protect them from permanent physical damage. In any case they needed the extra pesos. As they walked down the rows of tomato plants with their backpack sprayers, wearing no protective gear at all, they inadvertently sprayed each other as they passed on either side. Some had spraying rigs that leaked the chemicals down their backs. Elsewhere *banderilleros* stand in the fields waving their flags to direct the oncoming bush planes with the chemical mist descending upon them time and again.

The companies for which these farmhands work and the land on which they toil are usually Mexican, but as much as 90 percent of the financing comes from U.S. banks, and many of the producers are really just *prestanombres* or national stand-ins for U.S. growers and packers.[125] Others are subcontractors for California agribusiness firms or for such multinationals as Campbell's or Castle & Cooke.

Most of these Mixtec Indians are the second or third generation of migrants from the southern state of Oaxaca who fled their overpopulated and eroded homelands for farmworker jobs in the north.[126] Lucio Rojas left his mountain village in Oaxaca, Mexico's poorest state, fifteen years ago with his father and seven brothers. After leaving the economic desperation of their Oaxacan home, they worked for two years in Sinaloa, the state that produces more than half of the country's vegetable exports to the United States. Then they made their way to the San Quintín Valley, which was just beginning to experience its agricultural boom. There they formed the backbone of a farmworker organizing effort that helped raise wages for the Mixtec laborers—at least half of whom are women—while at the same time forcing the government and growers to grant the farmworker community land and sanitation services. Today the Rojas family lives in a largely Mixtec settlement named after Lucio Rojas' brother, a leader of the farmworker union who was killed by vigilantes in the fight to secure land for the Indian farmworkers.

Like others, Lucio Rojas has not stopped seeking opportunity. Although conditions have been much improved by the organizing work of the Independent Union of Farm Workers and Peasants (CIOAC), better wages and working conditions are still found north of the border. Returning home to San Quintín on the weekends, Lucio Rojas works during the week as a field foreman for an agricultural concern in San Diego's North County area.

One weekend when he was at home with his family in San Quintín, Rojas visited the estates where he used to work and the squalid housing where he and his family formerly lived. Posing as an evangelical leader, he gained easy access to the strawberry farms and the corresponding labor camps.

Here was the dark underside of the international agricultural production system. Hundreds of men, women, and children were picking strawberries and packing them into boxes marked with the labels of California agribusinesses. After working all day in the adjoining fields, the workers retired to the converted poultry sheds where they live. Drift from pesticide spraying routinely blows over the sheds, where in their desperation families use discarded pesticide drums for water storage.

Open borders for international trade—especially when pesticide controls are also loosened—increases the threat of a circle of poison. But to concentrate only on pesticide residues on the $2.5 billion in agricultural produce (about half of which are fruits and vegetables) shipped north annually to the U.S. market misses other more serious environmental hazards associated with transborder and global economic production. In the San Quintín Valley, as throughout northern Mexico, foreign and Mexican companies are producing cheap fruits and vegetables by paying farm laborers starvation wages and carelessly exposing them to acutely and chronically toxic chemicals.

More than a circle of poison, it seems like a two-way street, with dead ends on each side. From the south comes a steady stream of immigrants, crossing the border with hopes of better wages and a better working environment. At the same time, more companies are heading south with their capital, seeking cheaper production costs and a less restrictive regulatory climate. But north of the border there are fewer jobs and rents are prohibitively expensive, forcing many migrants to live under plastic tarps in the hills and canyons of Southern California. To the south, the repercussions of nonsustainable agricultural practices and the overreliance on agrochemicals place new limits on growth. Both in San Quintín and on the other side of the Sea of Cortez in the Hermosillo area, the end of the agricultural boom is already in sight as underground water supplies are drained and the sea water seeps in, killing the crops. As was the case earlier with the demise of cotton production in many parts of northern Mexico, the pests are becoming resistant even to the most toxic chemical cocktails that are being thrown at them, thereby threatening the continued viability of monocultural vegetable and fruit production in some areas.[127]

Increasingly pesticides are becoming a subject of international dispute. No longer is it automatically accepted that chemical saturation is essential for modern agricultural development. In the United States the market for chemical-free food is booming at the same time that the aftertaste of pesticide dependence is being increasingly recognized. In California the EPA has found that a fifth of the wells are contaminated by pesticides, and the late United Farm Worker's leader César Chávez had protested the immediate and long-term health effects of working with acutely poisonous chemicals. Meanwhile, the evidence is mounting in favor of the economic viability of organic farming and integrated pest-management practices that rely on natural predators and other less toxic methods to combat insect plagues.[128] Consumer concern has given rise to a small but expanding organic farming industry in Mexico to supply natural-foods stores and restaurants in the United States.[129]

As border trade barriers break down, the expanding community of environmentalists is demanding that global pesticide regulations be strengthened, not harmonized downward. "The notion that 'harmonized' maximum levels of protection should be enshrined in GATT [General Agreement on Tariffs and Trade] regulations is inappropriate at a time when farmers and governments are acknowledging that alternative farming methods can vastly reduce the use of chemical inputs," observed Monica Moore of the Pesticide Action Network.[130] In keeping with expanding consciousness of common responsibility for global ecological health, support is building in Congress for a measure that would ban the export of all chemicals prohibited for use in the United States and would require importers to tell customs officials what pesticides were used on produce destined for the U.S. market. Most advocates of free trade denounce such proposals as creating new obstacles to the free flow of goods across international borders, and Jay Vroom, president of the national Agricultural Chemicals Association, has called it "environmental imperialism."[131]

In Mexico, too, pesticides have become a matter of public debate. As in the United States, agrochemicals initially signaled the opening of the door to a brave new world of agricultural modernization characterized by cheaper and more abundant food. This new age started with the agricultural research sponsored by the Rockefeller Foundation in the early 1940s. But the promise held out by the Green Revolution for greater food self-sufficiency and for a more developed rural economy was only partially realized. Instead the Green Revolution heralded an increasing emphasis on an export-oriented and capitalist-controlled agricultural system that depended on new seed varieties requiring plenty of water, fertilizer, and chemical pesticides. By the 1960s traditional peasant agriculture was being pushed aside by what one author called "strawberry imperialism."[132] In places like El Bajío and the Culiacán Valley food crops such as corn and beans, and the small producers of those crops, were pushed out of the way in the drive to increase agroexports to the United States. Vegetable and fruit production for export depends heavily on chemical inputs, which are commonly applied twenty or more times a season to guarantee the cosmetic quality of the produce.

Even as the pressure to increase exports to the United States intensifies, the alarm is sounding in Mexico about the resulting environmental havoc and occupational hazards.[133] At universities throughout the country investigators are cataloging the consequences of this chemical dependency. At the College of Sonora one investigator reports cancer clusters in communities repeatedly exposed to aerial spraying.[134] Another researcher estimates that 90 percent of the food in Mexico, where there is no enforcement of food safety regulations, is contaminated.[135]

At his office in downtown Mexicali Professor Jesús Román Calleros of the Colegio de la Frontera Norte commented on the acrid smell in the air of the city. Calleros, an international water specialist, remarked that "with the summer wind from the south [Mexicali Valley agricultural area] and the winter wind from the north [Imperial Valley of California], Mexicali is continually covered with pesticides, and as a result we all seem to be suffering from allergies."[136]

Pesticide spray is a major problem in Mexicali, but not all the chemical threat comes from the surrounding agricultural valley. As an industrial center, the border city is also the site of several chemical companies, including at least one pesticide manufacturer. In January 1992 a 50,000-liter tank at the Química Orgánica pesticide-manufacturing plant (owned by the Mexican conglomerate CYDSA) ruptured, sending thirty-seven neighbors to the hospital from the noxious fumes and forcing the evacuation of nearby *colonias*. The incident came on the heels of fire at a pesticide plant in Córdoba, Veracruz, that provoked a catastrophic release of pesticide fumes. Contrary to an international agreement signed in 1983 by the United States and Mexico requiring notification of border environmental incidents, the Mexican environmental agency SEDUE did not alert the EPA. Instead the responsibility for cross-border environmental communication fell to two activist nongovernmental organizations, the Civil Committee for Ecological Disclosure in Mexicali and the Border Ecology Project in Naco, Arizona. As a result of strong citizen protests, the plant was closed.

Shutting down Química Orgánica has not solved the allergy epidemic in Mexicali nor cleared away the chemical mist, but it is a sign that questions about pesticide production and use are becoming public policy issues. More than simply a matter of agricultural modernization and cosmetic quality, the trade in pesticides and contaminated produce raises larger questions about the human rights of farmworkers, sustainable agricultural practices, ecological diversity, and cross-border environmental responsibility.

The Border as a Wasteland

Along with questions of food safety and the pesticide trade, the transboundary flow of hazardous wastes is also becoming a prominent public concern on both sides of the border. The focus has been on two problems of increasing magnitude: the dumping of U.S. wastes in Mexico and the disposal of the wastes created by the maquila industry.

There is no inventory of illegal hazardous waste dumps throughout Mexico.[137] Nor is there an informed estimate of the amount of chemicals exported from the United States for clandestine disposal. But there are plenty of indications that the practice of shipping hazardous wastes to Mexico is widespread—even though Mexico does not license dumps to handle foreign-produced wastes.[138]

In 1981 Mexican officials indicted a U.S. citizen for illegally dumping 160 drums of chemical waste, including forty-two drums of PCBs, at a clandestine site in the state of Zacatecas.[139] In the border community of Tecate, Mexican authorities found 10,000 gallons of heavy hydrocarbons and other toxic wastes that had been turned over to an unlicensed Mexican recycling company by several U.S. firms. Apparently on their way to a clandestine site in Chihuahua, four trucks carrying 175 barrels of PCBs were found parked two blocks from the border by El Paso authorities in 1989.

For companies facing disposal costs from $300 to $1,000 a barrel for toxic wastes in the United States, the possibility of paying $40 for dumping or "recycling" in Mexico is attractive indeed. Soaring disposal costs in the United States and the shrinking number of landfills have encouraged some firms to choose clandestine dumping south of the border. The ease with which vehicles can enter Mexico makes illegal dumping of U.S. wastes a low-risk gamble. On the U.S. side the chances of being detected are remote since U.S. Customs normally does not check the cargo but only the accompanying paperwork, which is easily doctored.[140] In the view of William Carter, a Los Angeles deputy district attorney specializing in environmental crimes, unscrupulous firms and waste haulers consider Mexico "a big trash can."[141] Carter estimated that tens of thousands of gallons of toxins flow south from California to Mexico each month. The rising costs of disposing wastes in the United States have increased clandestine cross-border dumping in Mexico. "The bottom line is greed and money," said an environmental crimes investigator in California.[142]

To discourage illegal toxic dumping either in California or in Mexico, the California Highway Patrol has a squad of "green cops." In one celebrated case, the green cops caught a California "wastelord" red-handed in a 1988 scheme to smuggle fifty-five-gallon drums of toxic chemicals across the border. Ray's Industrial Waste contracted with an aluminum corporation in the town of Torrance to dispose of fifty-seven barrels of hazardous wastes for a $12,000 fee. But instead of legally disposing the load, the owner paid a Mexican accomplice $30 a barrel to store the wastes in a dilapidated warehouse in Tijuana. When Mexican and U.S. officials searched the site, which is only yards from an elementary school, they found that it was filled with leaking barrels of toxic trash, including some marked "highly flammable." Reflecting on his job, green cop Gary Hanson said, "I think of these cases as investigating homicides. Only we're trying to break them twenty or thirty years in advance."[143]

It has been estimated that each North American citizen generates one ton of toxic waste every year.[144] Ironically, the expanding clout of environmentalists in the United States and other industrialized countries has contributed to the export of hazardous wastes to third world countries, both legally and illegally.[145] To counter this trend, environmental organizations like Greenpeace have mounted new educational and organizing campaigns aimed at stopping the north-south flow of toxics. But as Jim Vallette, the waste trade coordinator for Greenpeace, pointed out, "The only real solution to the toxic waste problem is to reduce the waste at its source—to stop it from ever being produced."[146]

Cross-border dumping of hazardous wastes is only a minor part of the hazardous waste menace facing Mexico. Industrialization has been Mexico's chosen model of development for more than a half-century, but little attention has been given until recently to ensuring that industrial wastes are disposed of properly. When Mexico opened its northern border in 1965 to U.S. assembly plants, virtually no safeguards were put in place to protect the environment and the population from the toxic substances that the firms brought with them. The government did provide the companies with water and electricity, but waste disposal facilities apparently were not a priority—either for the government or the maquiladoras.

Initially, hazardous wastes were not a serious problem since many of the early maquiladoras were garment industries. But the diversification into electronics, electrical components, chemicals, automotive, and other high-tech industries has resulted in the predominance of those sectors most likely to use hazardous substances.[147] In recent years, the fastest-growing segments of the maquila sector have been the chemical, furniture, automotive, and electronics industries.

More than a quarter-century after the maquila program was launched, there is widespread concern in the borderlands that uncontrolled dumping may be converting the region into another Love Canal. In 1990 spot sampling of wastewater discharges at twenty-three maquiladora sites by the Boston-based National Toxic Campaign confirmed these fears. Laboratory tests revealed that 75 percent of the sites tested were contaminated with highly toxic wastes. A water sample taken near one GM-owned plant showed a concentration of xylene that was 6,300 times higher than the standard for U.S. drinking water. An employee told one of the scientists that the company routinely flushes untreated solvents down the drain.[148] Explaining just how contaminated the region's water is, Marco Kaltofen of the National Toxic Campaign Fund said that if one were to try to duplicate the sampling, one would have to "drain a couple of cups from the bottom of your hot water tank where it gets lots of iron, add four or five tablespoons of used motor oil, spray in every aerosol can from your house, and add a little Dráno for taste."

The U.S. Department of Commerce keeps excellent statistics on U.S. exports and imports, but no government agency—in either the United States or Mexico—has been keeping track of the transboundary flow of hazardous substances. Although hundreds of thousands of tons of toxins travel to Mexico each year, neither country has a record of them. After the chemicals are used in the production process, they are disposed of in a variety of ways. For the most part, it seems, they simply drain out of the plants into the ditches, arroyos, and streams that run past the plants.

Since there have been no requirements that companies pre-treat their industrial wastes, many companies drain their wastes into city sewer systems or into open ditches. Even in Mexican cities such as Matamoros that do have wastewater treatment systems, the facilities are designed to treat human wastes, not toxic substances. As a result, toxic pollutants pass directly through these systems into the ecosystem. Moreover, the toxins knock out the biological treat-ment balance of the sewage treatment plants by killing the micro-or-ganisms that neutralize fecal contamination.[149]

A 1983 U.S.-Mexico accord requires that the maquiladoras re-turn their wastes to the country of origin or have them recycled in Mexico. Few U.S.-owned maquiladoras have returned their wastes to the United States. According to EPA records, fewer than 1 percent of the maquiladoras reported sending their hazardous wastes back to the United States in 1988.[150] Instead of returning the wastes to the United States, most have either left the barrels of chemicals in back lots or handed them over to local recycling industries. Because of increased public and official concern, U.S. firms have begun returning substantially more of their hazardous wastes to the United States since 1990.

Unlike the United States, Mexico has no maximum ninety-day storage rule, and it is common to see stacks of rusting, and often leaking, barrels piling up behind plants. Many of the "recyclers" or *materialistas* contracted by the maquiladoras are of question-able integrity. Instead of taking the wastes to an authorized dump or processing facility, the *materialistas* load up their pickups and take barrels to some clandestine desert spot for illegal disposal.[151] Reacting to stricter enforcement by the Mexican authorities, some maquiladoras are buying all their chemicals in Mexico or are paying duties on imported chemicals—thereby avoiding the reexportation requirement.[152]

Mexico is working to create a stronger waste-management program, but it has a long way to go. The government does not yet know the number of maquiladoras that generate hazardous wastes, the amount of waste generated, or the final disposition of that waste.[153] In 1990 SEDUE estimated that about half of the approximately 2,000 maquiladoras generate toxic wastes, but only some 300 had provided the agency with the required waste manifests.[154] But the manifests are exceedingly vague in that they often do not even specify the exact toxic substance being imported. In 1990 SEDUE estimated that only 30 percent of maquila reports on waste generation in Baja California provided enough information to be of any value.[155]

This reflects the fierce resistance on the part of the maquila industry to share information about the quantity and nature of the chemical substances they use. The lack of right-to-know provisions for communities and workers in Mexico helps keep this information from becoming public knowledge. Mexicans are not the only ones being kept in the dark about the transboundary flow of hazardous wastes. Although more regulations are on the books in the United States, the EPA does not have the capacity to monitor the disposal of maquila toxins. The nearest EPA office to the western border is in San Francisco, where the team tracking the hazardous wastes of the entire maquila industry consists of just one person.[156]

Finding itself in the international spotlight, the maquila industry has begun to improve its waste disposal practices. After media publicity about its illegal dumping and lack of the most elementary waste treatment facilities, General Motors decided in 1991 to install water treatment facilities at its thirty-five plants in Mexico. Increasingly, maquila trade associations are prodding their members to comply with government environmental regulations.

Mexico is sadly lacking in hazardous waste sites. It was not until 1981 that the country's first toxic dumps were opened, but these do not meet U.S. standards, and their capacity is not even adequate to meet the needs of domestic industries. Although the government is attempting to expand its waste management capacity, there are only a few commercial hazardous waste dumps in the entire country and only one full-service disposal facility. Fewer than a dozen companies are authorized to handle toxic wastes.[157] In Hermosillo, the location of a major Ford manufacturing plant, the industrial waste dump is located less than a half-mile uphill from the city's drinking-water supply. Recently, especially since the beginning of the free trade negotiations, the Mexican government has begun to clamp down on clandestine dumping. But as Tijuana's chief of sanitation said, "The creation of clandestine dumps is uncontrollable, since one or more new ones appear every day."[158] One company, Precision Microelectronics, shut down in 1989, leaving 142 employees without pay and some 800 gallons of toxins behind. The barrels were marked with the warning in English *Inhalation of Concentrated Vapors Can Be Fatal* and were stored only yards away from a Juárez neighborhood.

The EPA and SEDESOL have promised to install a computer database and tracking system to ensure that the toxic chemicals used by the maquila industry are properly disposed of. But data entry does not seem like much of a step forward to communities directly affected by hazardous wastes from border industries. They already know what the plants do with their wastes. In many cases the companies are dumping the wastes in their front yards. For the past ten years the people of Chilancingo, a Tijuana *colonia* of 25,000—mostly maquila workers—have seen a forty-eight-inch drainpipe spew chemical-laced water down on their homes when rains flood the waste ponds of the companies that sit above Chilancingo on Otay Mesa. It is not a daily occurrence, but when the water does come shooting over the mesa it spills wastes containing lead, copper, chrome, zinc, and cadmium onto the rutted streets in which children play.[159]

Some worry about the potential of a Bhopal-like accident along the border. In Matamoros that fear is focused on the multinational Química Flúor, a hydrogen fluoride factory partly owned by Du Pont that was previously given government permission to locate in an existing residential neighborhood. Concerned that an accident might endanger the neighborhoods surrounding the plant, President Salinas in 1991 created an "Intermediate Safeguard Zone" around the plant. The decree halts additional settlements within a 1.25-mile radius of the chemical plant's central smokestack.[160] Tens of thousands of poor Mexicans already live within the danger belt, and many have demanded that the plant be moved to a more deserted location. Joining the debate, U.S. environmental groups have charged that the imposition of a safety zone around the plant and the forced relocation of area residents rather than the plant itself are other indicators that all is not well with Mexico's regulatory system.[161]

Closely related to the threat to public health created by the irresponsible chemical dumping practices of the maquiladoras are the health and safety hazards faced by the maquila work force. Government and industry on both sides of the border have proved more willing to address public concerns about environmental deterioration than to negotiate occupational health standards. Roberto Sánchez of the Colegio de la Frontera Norte in Tijuana speculates that proposals to improve worker health constitute more of a threat to industrial production than do environmental protection measures. Problems of worker health have also received less media attention and are therefore not seen as a major obstacle to liberalized trade and investment.[162]

A study by the National Safe Workplace Institute concluded that many U.S. companies in Mexico do not enforce the occupational and environmental standards normal to U.S.-based operations. "We found that workers are seldom given training, that machinery is not safeguarded, and that instructions on chemical hazards are nearly always written in English. Work-related injuries and illnesses are typically ignored and workers who complain are typically discharged." The institute also found that the work pace is faster and the hours longer than in the United States.[163]

Workplace accidents are more common in Mexico than in the United States. In 1989 there were twenty-six incidents of partial amputations at factories in Nogales. Altogether there were 2,000 accidents in Nogales maquiladoras—about three times the rate experienced at comparable factories in the United States.[164] Whereas Mexico is moving fast to develop emissions and other environmental standards, there has been little progress on regulating air concentration levels and improving occupational health standards in Mexican factories.[165]

For roughly a dollar an hour, maquila workers become the human factor in fast-paced assembly processes that commonly result in back pain, eye strain, conjunctivitis, carpal tunnel syndrome, and mind-numbing boredom. From contact with hazardous substances, workers complain of skin rashes, nausea, and other physical reactions to the chemicals used in their jobs.[166] A lack of protective clothing and of access to information about workplace hazards is also common. In one factory women work with lead solder forty-eight hours every week, but few of them can read the labels warning that lead can cause birth defects and advising workers to wash their hands before eating or smoking. Workers experiencing unusual or persistent health problems such as breathing difficulty, stomach problems, or sudden emotional changes are sometimes told by company doctors that their problems are psychological.[167]

Occupational health problems are by no means limited to factories south of the border, but Mexican workers are even less protected than their U.S. counterparts and do not have the same avenues to seek redress through the legal system. An interesting case in this respect is that of GTE Lenkurt in Albuquerque, New Mexico, where a group of workers and their attorneys were awarded $2 million to $3 million in 1987 for health problems, including cancer, neurological damage, and numerous hysterectomies, resulting from their exposure to chemical compounds in the electronics factory. In 1982 GTE Lenkurt decided to transfer the bulk of the most hazardous jobs to its plant in Juárez after experiencing years of worker protests and complaints of unsafe working conditions. Although the peso devaluation in Mexico was probably the main factor in the decision to relocate, worker discontent also played a part.[168]

It would be wrong to conclude, however, that the maquiladoras treat their workers worse than do domestic industries in Mexico. The assembly plants, despite all their problems, may be among the safest and cleanest places to work in Mexico's manufacturing sector. Although complaints about few rest periods, exposure to toxins, excessive noise levels, repetitive assembly work, and insufficient training seem to indicate a careless attitude about workplace safety on the part of maquila management, many workers credit the maquiladoras for providing meals, educational and sports programs, and some medical services.

According to one study, the rate of maquila workers reporting backaches, headaches, and dizziness was not greater than the rate of employees in service industries in Tijuana.[169] Such surveys do not, however, reveal possible long-term health problems, such as cancer and birth defects, resulting from regular and relatively uncontrolled exposure to hazardous chemical compounds used by many of the maquila industries. As it is, there is not enough epidemiological evidence to form any overall conclusions about the severity of the occupational health climate inside the maquiladoras. The industry has fiercely resisted most studies of worker health and safety by denying researchers access to the factories and company records.[170]

Among the proponents and advocates of free trade, a debate rages about the significance of environmental and occupational health factors in influencing plant relocation. On the face of it, logic would seem to be with those who argue that the higher environmental and worker safety regulations enforced in the United States play a major role in driving companies out of the country to "pollution havens" such as Mexico. Already the amount that U.S. firms spend on controlling pollution is one of the highest in the world, and loose enforcement of environmental regulations in Mexico makes such high expenditures unnecessary.

A recent study by a New Mexico State University professor found that the growth rates of nine maquiladora industries over the 1982-1990 period were highly correlated with those industries' pollution abatement costs in the United States.[171] And according to a survey by the Colegio de la Frontera Norte in Tijuana, about 10 percent of the maquiladoras surveyed cited environmental regulations as a primary factor in company decisions to leave the United States. Another 17 percent considered environmental regulations an important factor.[172]

These findings are controversial, however. The Office of the U.S. Trade Representative claims that the pollution-haven argument advanced by environmentalists and labor unions in their opposition to more liberalized global trading is spurious.[173] Backing its claim that environmental compliance costs are not a deciding factor in plant relocation decisions, the Office of the U.S. Trade Representative cites numerous academic studies and its own data.[174]

According to most academic studies, it does appear that environmental and occupational health compliance costs are usually not the deciding factor in investment relocation for most large corporations. Only in the case of major polluters and smaller firms are these considerations an important reason to relocate.[175] There is also strong evidence that most transnational corporations are increasingly seeking to standardize their operations throughout the world, with the result that their foreign branches usually abide by higher environmental and worker-safety standards than domestically owned companies.[176] Increasingly, when large corporations make capital investments they anticipate rising standards and find the old, highly polluting equipment and technology are unprofitable when compared with modern, clean technology that conserves materials and energy.[177] Other studies have demonstrated no widespread pollution-driven relocation of U.S. industries except in a few highly toxic industries such as asbestos manufacture or those producing such metals as copper, zinc, and lead.[178]

This is not to say that other firms do not consider the advantages of less government regulation in their relocation decisions but only that in many cases these may not be as critical as nonenvironmental factors, such as labor costs, production strategies, and global marketing plans. In the case of agricultural companies, longer growing seasons and the lack of freezes are also major siting considerations.

Even if most companies do not intentionally seek pollution havens, this does not mean that they maintain the same environmental and worker safety standards once they have located abroad. In fact, a double standard between U.S.-based firms and their foreign branches is common worldwide. This has certainly been the case in Mexico, where maquiladoras have ignored the most basic environmental and occupational health standards. A study sponsored by the International Labor Organization found that the home-based operations of transnational corporations generally had better health and safety performance than those of their foreign branches and subsidiaries, particularly those located in less developed countries such as Mexico.[179]

Although most U.S.-based transnational corporations are not relocating to Mexico to avoid pollution-abatement costs, these costs may be an important consideration for some major companies. Eastman Kodak, two of whose plants were named among the top twenty emitters of air toxins in the United States, is setting up new plants in Mexico along with other high-tech chemical and electronics manufacturers.[180] The fact that at least five Firestone workers had contracted leukemia and that unsafe exposure to benzene was suspected as the cause may have been the reason the company moved a tire plant from Salinas, California, to Mexico. As mentioned earlier, the fastest-growing industries in the maquila sector are ones where contamination, hazardous wastes, and occupational safety are major concerns. Liberalized foreign investment rules, particularly in the petroleum and petrochemical industries, are likely to attract an increasing number of U.S. chemical companies to Mexico.

Dozens of furniture companies in Southern California are clearly seeking a pollution haven on the other side of the border. Reacting to new controls in the South Coast region restricting the use of solvent-based paints and requiring the installation of spray chambers to contain fumes, at least forty furniture firms in the Los Angeles area have moved or are planning to move to Baja California. This flight southward by the furniture industry endangers a $1.3 billion industry and 63,000 workers in Southern California. Three percent of the hydrocarbon pollution in Los Angeles has been attributed to the paints, stains, and lacquers currently favored by woodworking companies.

Stricter air control regulations are not the only reasons companies like Fine Good Furniture are relocating. High workers' compensation bills in California and the cheaper labor costs across the border—about 13 percent of U.S. pay—have also pushed and pulled furniture firms toward Mexico.[181] In Mexico there is virtually no workers' compensation. And such companies as Muebles Fino Buenos (a translation of Fine Good Furniture) no longer must deal with the constant intrusions of air-quality inspectors, emissions monitors, and lawyers for aggrieved workers and neighbors of the polluting factory. In Los Angeles the factory owner paid tens of thousands of dollars in fines and penalties. But although the company's reincarnation in Tijuana is easily meeting local environmental standards, neighbors of Muebles Fino Buenos complain of dizziness, sore throats, nausea, and the smell of solvents all day long. The fine dust of lacquer settles over nearby homes and vehicles.[182]

Despite a dramatic improvement in Mexico's environmental regulations since 1988, Mexico has no established air-quality standard to regulate paint and solvent emissions. This lack of environmental and worker safety regulations helps explain the boom in the furniture industry along Mexico's northern border. As one factory owner acknowledged, "I can find lots of Mexican workers in the United States. What I can't find here in Tijuana is the government looking over my shoulder."[183] The number of furniture maquiladoras increased from fifty-nine in 1980 to 274 in 1990, with employment rising from 3,200 to 25,700 workers.[184] These runaway plants may only be postponing the day of reckoning if SEDESOL follows through with promises to bring its standards up to U.S. levels.[185] But relocating companies are betting that any upward harmonization of air-quality regulations to the strict standards of Southern California will be a long time coming.

The case of the furniture industry demonstrates that fears that Mexico serves as a pollution haven cannot be dismissed. When strict standards for asbestos manufacture took effect in the 1970s, companies set up new plants in Juárez and Agua Prieta. Border Ecology Project Director Dick Kamp, who lives in the Arizona border town of Naco, points to the Sonocal lime plant across the border as a case of what he wryly calls "low-grade technology transfer." In 1976, after the EPA shut down the then-U.S. facility for particulate noncompliance, it was purchased by Sonocal, which then packed up the plant and reassembled it on the other side of the border with no pollution control.[186] Mexico serves as a pollution haven for the U.S. firm, but the fine lime dust blows across the international border. Kamp, a leading advocate for the incorporation of strong environmental and occupational health standards into international trading agreements, is concerned that the lime dust is damaging the health of his children and other area residents.[187]

Chapter 4

Governments Face the Environment

The environment was largely ignored in official U.S.-Mexican relations until relatively recently. Toward the end of the 1970s, however, the environmental repercussions of being neighbors and the consequences of increased development along the border became more pressing concerns. As pollution levels climbed, border communities, environmentalists, and public health workers demanded government action. Moving into the 1990s, concerned citizens in each country also began urging their elected representatives to broaden the focus of joint efforts to include the Mexican interior. Much of the interior has already suffered from rapid, unplanned development, and although many areas are likely to experience increased pressure as U.S.-Mexican economic integration goes forward, these have mostly been ignored in joint environmental initiatives.

The U.S. and Mexican governments responded to the public outcry by concluding several agreements that address environmental problems. They also committed their environmental agencies to step up efforts to combat deteriorating environmental conditions. The effectiveness of these government responses to environmental contamination depends on political will, the resources available, and the quality of the institutions and agreements set up to coordinate joint action.

Unfortunately, policy and performance have remained out of step with government promises. With their attentions focused on economic objectives, the two governments have had other priorities besides solving environmental problems. Their development strategies have emphasized growth over sustainability—the careful stewardship of natural resources to ensure that future generations will be able to meet their own needs. More concerned about promoting economic growth than about regulating or taxing businesses to protect the environment, the two governments generally put off finding remedies to environmental problems caused by industrial development until pushed to do so by public pressure. Even then, they have balked at hiking taxes to make business pay for environmental programs.

Problems of political will and development strategy aside, resolving international environmental concerns is a complicated task with both technical and diplomatic features. Solving the problems requires comprehensive, binational planning and overcoming differences between U.S. and Mexican social, economic, political, and administrative systems. When soot from family fire pits in Juárez drifts across the river to El Paso, for example, solutions must deal realistically with the economic roots of the contamination and the political and social consequences of cleanup. The stark differences in wealth and other resources between the United States and Mexico are also evident in the limited financial and technical resources available to Mexico for attacking environmental problems.

In addition, the problems affect so many different communities, activist organizations, business groups, and government agencies that finding solutions is a tricky combination of confrontation and compromise. A multitude of local, state, and federal government agencies from both countries are responsible for monitoring environmental problems, devising solutions, and implementing them. At the federal level, the EPA, Mexico's SEDESOL, and the binational IBWC have primary authority for working on joint environmental problems. Their efforts are multiplied by state and local agencies, community groups, private organizations, businesses, and environmental organizations whose priorities and agendas frequently compete with those of the federal governments. In fact, these front-line institutions often find themselves at odds with their own federal agencies over the pace, scope, and financing of environmental projects, while working more closely with counterparts across the border.

Also bogging down the search for solutions to shared environmental woes are questions about who is to blame for the problems and who will pay to solve them. Because much of the pollution along the border emanates from the Mexican side, U.S. policy makers and taxpayers have often fought against paying big bills for cleanup or infrastructure development. And taxpayers rightfully question why they should foot the bill for pollution caused by U.S. businesses that have moved to Mexico and profited from lax environmental standards and concessionary tax and tariff policies.

Increasingly, however, communities and government officials in both countries appear to be realizing that finger pointing is a waste of time and that common solutions to the mounting catastrophe are needed. But coming to an agreement about how much of the cost is to be paid by the United States or Mexico, by local, state, or federal revenues, and by businesses or private citizens is a ticklish political challenge.

Border communities in both countries are typically too strapped financially to generate the funds required for large environmental and infrastructure projects. They depend on support from state and federal governments that is often inadequate and slow in coming. In the United States, for instance, decisions about national appropriations are made in the U.S. Congress. States located away from the border area are reluctant to chip in for environmental protection programs that do not benefit their own citizens. In Mexico funds for border projects generally have come from the federal government, which has had only limited resources for environmental programs. Until public pressure in the United States mounted because of the NAFTA negotiations, the Mexican government prioritized cleanup in Mexico City and paid scant attention to border problems.

But the reality of U.S.-Mexico integration means that for practical and ethical reasons, costs must be divided among sectors in both countries. The problems along the border are a direct result of industrial integration between the two countries and environmental protection will benefit communities on both sides of the line.[188] Governments—whether local, state, or federal—and private actors in both Mexico and the United States have promoted the development strategies whose effects are endangering the environment. With development have come strains on the infrastructure and natural resources that are the responsibilities of public and private parties in both countries.

Free trade will add a new complexity to U.S.-Mexico environmental relations. While the border was a logical focus of common concern before NAFTA, a free trade agreement would sharply expand the territory in Mexico that is affected by U.S.-Mexico economic integration and that is subject to rapid development. Energy and resource consumption, pesticide use, hazardous waste production, and vehicle and industrial emissions are expected to increase in the Mexican interior if the free trade pact is ratified. Rapid urbanization and heightened infrastructure pressures are also expected, as government policies squeeze small farmers out of rural areas and people rush to the cities hopeful of employment. Until all these problems are confronted adequately, the future economic and environmental vitality of the entire region will be threatened.

Building the Joint Environmental Framework

Water sanitation problems along the border were the first environmental issues to draw attention from both the U.S. and Mexican governments. Efforts to deal with these problems—primarily through monitoring water quality and constructing wastewater treatment facilities—go back to the 1940s. The vehicle for resolving these problems was the U.S.-Mexico International Boundary and Water Commission (IBWC). Composed of a U.S. section and its Mexican counterpart, the Comisión Internacional de Límites y Aguas, the IBWC is one of the few institutions created by the two countries that is binational in structure and not just in rhetoric.[189]

The IBWC grew out of the first truly binational U.S.-Mexico institution. The International Boundary Commission was set up by treaty in 1889 to resolve disputes over the location of the boundary between the two countries. Over the years the organization's authority expanded to include boundary water problems. The Water Treaty of 1944 renamed the body and added water supply and quality issues to the commission's mandate. It was not until the late 1970s, however, that mounting public criticism of water quality in the borderlands prodded the IBWC to broaden its responsibility over a wide range of water pollution issues.[190]

As was the case with water pollution, cooperation between the United States and Mexico on other environmental issues moved forward in the 1970s. These first efforts were halting and incomplete, however, in part because the Mexican government had decreed some general environmental principles but had not set standards for enforcement. At the same time, formal responsibility for protecting the Mexican environment was assigned to a low level in the Ministry of Health.

But increasing environmental awareness and concern in Mexico helped the government step up its own programs, and growing demands from border communities spurred the United States and Mexico to expand joint programs. In 1978 the EPA and Mexico's environmental subsecretariat signed a Memorandum of Understanding committing the two agencies to work together on environmental problems. Although the agreement was flawed in various ways, it was a milestone because it was the first comprehensive attempt to approach environmental problems on a joint basis.[191] Targeting pollution control and abatement and promising information exchanges, annual meetings, consultations, policy coordination, and the establishment of parallel projects, the memorandum anticipated the framework of later agreements.[192] Beginning in the early 1980s, the United States and Mexico intensified their joint approach to environmental problems, producing a flurry of agreements over the next ten years.[193]

The effectiveness of U.S.-Mexico environmental programs has depended in part on the quality of the institutions set up to carry them out. Although the EPA has never had the funding or authority needed to carry out a full-scale program of environmental protection, Mexico's institutions have been even weaker and more politicized. When President de la Madrid established the Secretariat of Urban Development and Ecology (SEDUE) in 1982, the move seemed to signal a strengthening of Mexican environmental policies.

With SEDUE's creation, responsibility for environmental protection no longer rested in a low-level agency attached to the health ministry. Instead, SEDUE was a cabinet-level ministry with all the authority of its predecessor as well as new responsibilities over housing, public works, and agricultural and water policy.[194] Authority over many environmental programs was centralized in the new secretariat, which, in becoming the country's lead agency for environmental issues, assumed an oversight and coordinating role over the environmental activities of other agencies—at least on paper.

Thus strengthened, SEDUE signed a broad-ranging environmental accord with the EPA in 1983. Where the 1978 memorandum had represented a handshake between two lower-level agencies in each country, the 1983 framework agreement, commonly called the La Paz agreement, was a presidential-level accord that resulted from a summit meeting between then-presidents Ronald Reagan and Miguel de la Madrid.

Designed as a broad framework within which the United States and Mexico could confront shared environmental problems on the border, the La Paz agreement was purposely written in general terms. It named the EPA and SEDUE as the lead agencies in handling joint environmental issues but reaffirmed the IBWC's jurisdiction over water pollution along the border. Follow-up agreements, known as annexes, committed the two countries to work on specific problems, such as sewerage needs in Tijuana. Between 1983 and 1992, the EPA and SEDUE appointed binational working groups on water, air, hazardous waste, emergency response, enforcement, and pollution prevention as authorized by the annexes. These groups were authorized to investigate problems under their jurisdiction and devise joint solutions.

The La Paz agreement represented a big step forward for U.S.-Mexico environmental protection efforts. It helped clear up questions about which agencies were responsible for which problems by specifying the jurisdictions of the IBWC, the EPA, and SEDUE. Flexible and inclusive, it provided a mechanism for the two governments to reach agreement on whichever environmental questions they chose to take up. More than under any previous arrangement, federal agencies were encouraged to cooperate with local, state and nongovernmental actors on transboundary environmental problems. Finally, in designating the border area as a strip of land that extended 100 kilometers (about 62 miles) on either side of the actual U.S.-Mexico boundary, the agreement recognized the integrated reality of the border region.

But like the 1978 memorandum, the La Paz agreement has a number of serious weaknesses.[195] Because it is an executive agreement and not a treaty, implementation is left to the discretion of the two governments. The agreement is neither binding nor enforceable. Although it provides a framework for cooperation and coordination, its nontreaty status means that the governments are not obligated to use it or to follow through on decisions made subsequent to it. Its success therefore depends heavily on the political commitments of the incumbent administrations in each country. Perhaps reflecting the half-hearted zeal of the two governments, the programs resulting from the La Paz agreement have not received adequate funding. This crucial shortcoming means that the responsible agencies have never been funded to carry out a thorough program of needs assessment or enforcement, much less border cleanup, pollution prevention, and resource conservation.

Winning NAFTA with Environmental Promises

Economics and politics, not the environment, have prompted the burst of joint environmental initiatives undertaken after 1990. As the two governments moved a free trade agreement to the tops of their priority lists in the late 1980s, public concerns about potential environmental impacts threatened to derail the accord. The governments responded with a series of high-profile initiatives that built on the La Paz agreement and other earlier efforts at environmental protection and binational cooperation. While those attempts had looked good on paper, they had been poorly implemented, a fact that the two governments said they were going to correct with the new initiatives.

Until the NAFTA negotiations got under way, SEDUE was known as a politicized operation that was lax about enforcing the country's environmental regulations. Beset by corruption and patronage, the troubled agency had few trained personnel and never received the full support of the government.[196]

This picture began to change when Mexico and the United States began barreling toward the free trade agreement. SEDUE's budget increased significantly after 1989, expanding by some 613 percent by 1991. Whereas in 1989 Mexico was spending about 8 cents per person on environmental activities, by 1991 that figure had increased to 48 cents. Even so, SEDUE's budget was still inadequate—only $39 million in 1991—and funding was sought from outside sources, including the World Bank, Japan, and the United States, to help invigorate its programs.[197]

Bolstered by new funds and motivated by the need to convince U.S. policy makers that NAFTA would not further threaten the border environment, SEDUE enhanced its enforcement efforts. New inspectors were added, and sanctions—even plant shutdowns—were leveled against some environmental offenders, especially in Mexico City and along the border.[198]

There were two other major outcomes of the governments' efforts to win the support of legislators, environmentalists, and border communities for NAFTA. The Integrated Border Environmental Plan (IBEP) and the Environmental Review were released on the same day in February 1992. The border plan laid out a list of current border problems, especially those afflicting the largest sister cities. The Environmental Review was supposed to examine the effect of the proposed NAFTA on environmental conditions in Mexico, whether along the border or elsewhere. In reality, however, the Environmental Review also focused primarily on the border, with the exception of discussing a few other issues, like air pollution in Mexico City.

Formulated by the EPA and SEDUE, the border plan committed the United States and Mexico to cooperate on a variety of border environmental problems. As a subsidiary to the La Paz agreement, the plan inventoried many of the problems of the border region but left detailed programs for resolving the issues to be developed in subsequent agreements, similar to the minutes of the IBWC or the annexes of the La Paz accord. Topics covered included hazardous waste, emergency response, water supply and quality, air quality, housing and infrastructure, habitat protection, and municipal solid waste.

If the intent of the planners was to silence opposition to NAFTA, their hopes went unrealized. Activists, community residents, scholars, public health workers, and state and local government leaders blasted the IBEP for a string of shortcomings ranging from its vagueness to funding inadequacies and its avoidance of crucial issues.[199] They also criticized the plan for its reliance on the IBWC and for neglecting to look at the likely impacts of free trade on the border environment.[200] When, in the fall of 1991, communities all along the U.S.-Mexico border turned out to comment on the draft IBEP, the meeting rooms buzzed with anger from San Diego to Brownsville. "We knew we'd get creamed," said Sylvia Correa, the EPA's manager of Latin American programs. "But we wanted to hear what the people had to say."[201]

Response to the Environmental Review was even more critical.[202] As Lynn Fischer of the Natural Resources Defense Council put it, "The Environmental Review was a farce." Despite its mandate, Fischer said, the Environmental Review "didn't really look at the environmental impacts of free trade."[203] The review fell far short of safeguarding the environment by failing to outline enforcement mechanisms or recommend provisions to protect state and local standards from assault as barriers to free trade. This dissatisfaction with the IBEP and the Environmental Review was one reason why there is so great a demand along the border for a more thorough environmental impact statement of the proposed free trade agreement.

The joint environmental activities of the United States and Mexico reflect the limitations of these agreements. They emphasize education and information sharing as opposed to enforcement, and they are generally parallel instead of truly binational. In addition, funding inadequacies plague the programs, especially those involving infrastructure development at the local level.

Still, the two countries are cooperating on a range of activities, the need for which is undeniable. In recognition of the limited technical resources available in the country, training and technical assistance dominate the EPA's assistance to Mexico.[204] These include things like inspector trainings and technical presentations to help Mexico design vehicle inspection and auto emissions programs. The United States also funded an Environmental Technology Clearinghouse, known as Envirotech, a computerized data system that indexes more than 500 databases on pollution control and energy conservation technology available in the United States. According to the Environmental Review, the EPA will help Mexican develop environmental regulations and will work with Mexico on other issues, such as comparing pesticides and their usages and tolerances in Mexico to U.S. standards in order to resolve differences between the two countries.[205]

Under the authority of binational environmental agreements and the minutes of the IBWC, Mexico and the United States cooperate on informational programs, such as data collection, trainings, technology transfers, and needs assessments. Pollution-monitoring programs are also being set up. Although moving sluggishly, the two countries are working to provide wastewater treatment plants and sewage systems up and down the border. They also plan to devise a system for tracking shipments of hazardous materials from the United States into Mexico and for collecting data about how the waste by-products are disposed. This kind of information is not available at present and is greatly needed if enforcement efforts are to be enhanced.

But the example of the Inland Joint Response Team (JRT) highlights the fact that despite advances, the governments have not gone far enough with their cooperative initiatives. In 1988 the JRT was authorized to coordinate joint emergency response plans in case of natural disasters or accidental toxic releases along the border. Participating sister cities are supposed to create their own emergency response teams. Known as Local Emergency Planning Committees in the United States and as Local Committees on Mutual Assistance in Mexico, these teams are supposed to devise joint plans and interact together during emergencies. The need for such bodies is clear, but most have existed only on paper and have never received adequate funding. Those that do exist tend to function parallel to one another instead of in tight coordination. Their effectiveness is further limited by lack of training, little or no information about toxic substances in their communities, and inadequate border infrastructure such as bridges and water delivery systems.

Changing the Playing Field in Mexico

The restructuring of the Mexican government carried out under Salinas swept up the country's environmental protection agency in May 1992. At that time Salinas created a new super-ministry known as the Secretariat of Social Development (SEDESOL) and announced that many environmental functions would be decentralized and privatized. The restructuring of Mexico's environmental apparatus will surely affect the quality of joint U.S.-Mexico activities, although the changes are too recent to evaluate their effect.

But the way the new ministry has been structured raises many questions about just how effectively it will be able to safeguard the environment. At a symbolic level, protection of the environment has been visibly downgraded from SEDUE's cabinet-level ministry to the status of an agency within SEDESOL. Even SEDUE's former director, Patricio Chirinos, said the move would transform the environmental protection agency into a "second-floor institution."

Among other tasks, SEDESOL was charged with formulating environmental policy and enforcing Mexico's laws regarding the environment.[206] Two new bodies—the National Ecology Institute and the Attorney General's Office for the Protection of the Environment—were created within the new secretariat to handle analysis, policy development, and enforcement. Although some of SEDUE's environmental functions were passed on to different ministries—contributing to bureaucratic fragmentation—

SEDESOL retained control over the issues that had caused most public outcry in U.S. and Mexican constituencies with influence over the future of NAFTA. These functions included control over toxins and pollution problems in urban areas and on the border. SEDESOL also received authority over conservation programs and implementation of the border plan.[207]

Concerned observers fear that, in SEDESOL, one highly politicized and patronage-plagued institution—SEDUE—has been replaced by another that is even more highly politicized. SEDESOL's first director, Luis Donaldo Colosio, was a former head of the Institutional Revolutionary Party (PRI) and a major contender for the position of PRI presidential candidate for 1994.[208] His appointment suggests that the new ministry fills a political need for the ruling party. In addition to environmental programs, SEDESOL oversees another intensely politicized initiative, the National Solidarity Program (Pronasol), a public works program that funnels development projects and material assistance to the poor. The fact that environmental programs are subsumed under the same agency as Pronasol raises fears that environmentalism will be treated only as a political tool.

Along with SEDUE's dissolution, authority over environmental programs is being decentralized and privatized. Funded in part by a four-year World Bank loan, the process of "modernization" of Mexico's environmental regime and transfer of much authority to the states is to be complete by 1994. Mario Aguilar, SEDESOL's attaché to Washington, explained that under the changes, Mexican state and local governments will take on "concurrent authority" with the federal government over environmental problems.[209] They are authorized to write legislation and enact standards that can be "more, not less stringent" than federal legislation, Aguilar said, and they will be responsible for enforcing compliance with environmental regulations.

The sources of funding for the state and local programs were not identified in the restructuring plans, making it likely that Mexico's state and local governments will be unable to pursue their new programs. Even if the states and local governments write tough technical standards, their programs will lack real power unless their enforcement provisions are equally strict, which is not guaranteed under current plans. What is more, as long as Mexico's budgetary, administrative, and political systems remain centralized and dominated by the PRI, federal influence over environmental policies will remain intact.

Mexico is also privatizing many environmental functions. Under the new system, similar in many ways to that of the United States, private consultants and contractors will take over functions that once were handled by the government. These tasks include designing standards, monitoring pollution and compliance, licensing, and inspection.

Although privatization could improve efficiency, it increases the danger of corruption and conflict of interest. For example, a consultant to industry can legally act both as an approved plant inspector and as a consultant to a given firm.[210] Patronage in Mexico is commonly dispensed at the state and local levels, increasing the chances of corruption as these functions are privatized. In addition, the state and municipal governments do not have the expertise to supervise private contractors adequately. And in the short term at least, Mexico's environmental inspectors were being cut from the payroll, with some 48 percent of the inspector staff slated for elimination despite government promises to deploy new inspectors.[211]

Conflicting Viewpoints and Agendas

Resolving shared environmental problems is further complicated by the number of organizations and agencies that are affected and by their different needs and priorities. When the EPA San Diego-Tijuana Border Task Force meets to discuss water treatment initiatives, for example, some thirty representatives of agencies ranging from the U.S. Fish and Wildlife Service to the local health departments attend the gathering.

The involvement of all these different agencies complicates environmental planning. In the United States—and soon in Mexico if the decentralization goes as planned—much enforcement power is left to the states. States often devise their own regulations and standards on air pollution and pesticides or other toxins. Variations from state to state *within* the country can be extreme; the problem of coordination is even more severe with cross-border questions.

Tensions result, too, from the different agendas and needs of local areas and states versus the national perspectives of the federal governments. Despite whatever local presence they may achieve—which has been completely insufficient in most areas—

SEDESOL and the EPA represent federal viewpoints and must uphold strategies decided upon in the capital cities. The contradictions between the federal agendas and the needs of people living in the crisis zones and trying to respond to the problems there cause tensions among local, state, and national bodies. Both the EPA and SEDESOL, for example, were strong promoters of NAFTA during the negotiations, even though many border communities and local and state governments fought for stiffer environmental protections in the accord.

The welter of agencies involved in environmental issues has helped the federal governments pass responsibility for implementation, enforcement, and funding onto state and local governments. But state and local agencies in both countries find it hard to stretch their revenues to pay for needed improvements in infrastructure and environmental protection. This problem was compounded during the 1980s as federal dollars to states and municipalities dwindled with the recession in the United States and the economic crisis in Mexico. Washington's high-profile advocacy of expensive improvements in border environmental infrastructure has irritated border communities strapped for the funds such improvements would require.

In addition to problems like these, the initiatives being worked out at the federal level do not explicitly protect local and state environmental standards that might be stiffer than national or international norms. The Bush administration in particular had pushed for consistency with the principles being worked out in the ongoing round of negotiations of the GATT. If those principles are accepted at the negotiations, tough local and state standards will likely be preempted by international norms that reflect the lowest common denominator of protective standards agreed to by the many nations involved in the negotiations.

Policy–Performance Gap

The current level of U.S.-Mexico cooperation on environmental problems is unprecedented. Indeed, the two countries exchanged environmental attachés in the early 1990s, reflecting the importance and cordiality of the relationship. But even with all the joint programs, plans, and meetings, environmental problems and their negative health effects continue to accumulate.

One big problem is lax enforcement of environmental regulations. The problem has been especially severe in Mexico, which has usually tried to work out voluntary agreements with industry, rather than identify and levy penalties against violators. In many cases the country's environmental agencies simply lack the technical and financial resources to enforce monitoring and compliance requirements.

For whatever reasons, noncompliance with environmental regulations is widespread in the country, even though most of Mexico's laws and regulations are advanced. For example, the U.S. General Accounting Office found that in a sample of six of the 116 new U.S.-majority-owned maquiladoras that began operations in 1990 and 1991 none had prepared environmental impact assessments (EIAs) before starting up. This was true even though Mexican law requires new companies to submit EIAs before receiving operating permits. Even more telling, the Mexican agency that issues operating licenses allowed four of the six companies to start up before receiving applicable permits for air emissions, water discharges, and hazardous waste management. According to SEDESOL, noncompliance with EIA requirements is extensive throughout the country, not just in the maquiladoras.[212]

Cooperative agreements between the two countries compound these problems by relying on voluntary compliance. Carefully guarding sovereignty concerns, the agreements leave enforcement to the discretion of each country. Even the new working group on enforcement established under the La Paz agreement will primarily facilitate data collection, information exchanges, and occasional joint site visits "by invitation."

Because neither government is doing its part to enforce environmental regulations and safeguards, activist groups are picking up the slack. Instead of the governments doing their job of water and air monitoring and keeping track of hazardous wastes, these tasks have fallen to small citizens groups and environmental organizations like the Border Ecology Project in Naco, Arizona, and the Border Project for Environmental Education in Tijuana.[213] But the effectiveness of these groups is limited, at least in Mexico, because the country does not have right-to-know legislation to make sure that information about toxic materials and other potential environmental hazards is available to the public. Likewise,

Mexico has virtually no guarantees of public access to the courts to enforce administrative action against violators.

Another fundamental problem is the persistent failure of the two governments to provide adequate funding to resolve the massive environmental problems caused by rapid development and U.S.-Mexico economic integration. Because insufficient funds have been a major factor in Mexico's uneven progress on environmental concerns, this oversight is especially glaring. To make a good-faith attempt to carry out the programs outlined in the IBEP, for example, the U.S. and Mexican environmental agencies will surely have to expand their staffs, equip new offices, purchase and set up computer systems, modernize laboratories, and pay transportation expenses. But the plan did not even attempt to estimate the costs of its new programs, much less outline strategies for raising such funds.

The environmental initiatives of the United States and Mexico are also limited by their narrow focus, mostly on the border regions. But expected increases in trade and investment will affect areas deep in the Mexican interior. Environmental devastation is already common throughout Mexico, where deforestation, pollution, resource depletion, and biosphere degradation are by-products of poverty and development strategies. As the World Bank explained in 1992, Mexico suffers from "grave" environmental problems "exacerbated by several decades of industrialization without assessment of, or attention to, environmental costs."[214]

All these environmental pressures would likely worsen under a free trade accord, especially without a shift in development policies. The United States has provided some economic aid to Mexico for environmental and conservation programs in the interior—for monitoring air pollution in Mexico City, for instance—but little direct attention has been paid to these needs.

Government officials claimed that an agreement that would remedy these oversights as well as promote private sector involvement in pollution control would be signed. EPA Director William Reilly said that such an agreement would address issues like hazardous waste management and enforcement throughout the two countries, not just along the border.[215] But the promised agreement was never signed. Without such a commitment to deal with the array of Mexico's environmental problems, many environmental groups in both countries warn that Mexico may divert scarce resources from serious and growing problems in the interior to pump up programs on the border that are more visible to U.S. policy makers and activists.

Co-opting the Critics

When the governments of Mexico and the United States announced in 1990 their common intention to seek a free trade agreement, they knew that citizen concern about runaway plants seeking cheap Mexican labor was a major issue in the United States. But they probably were not expecting that approval of their free trade proposals would be threatened by such matters as black water, clandestine waste dumps, and lime dust. The poison trail running between the two nations suddenly became a major obstacle to free trade on the fast track.

Border communities, the labor movement, environmental organizations, and consumer groups in the United States joined together in demanding that their environmental concerns be addressed before any trade accord with Mexico be approved. Although not opposed to free trade, border communities quickly seized the opportunity of the trade negotiations with Mexico to focus attention on the festering infrastructural, environmental, and public health problems in the borderlands. But more than sympathy, the border communities wanted an injection of federal dollars for public-sector infrastructure projects such as wastewater treatment plants, water and sewage projects, and new roads and bridges. As the chairperson of the Border Trade Alliance, a business organization devoted to economic development of the borderlands, explained, "We who breathe the air and drink the water along the border are the first to say we support free trade and that we also want a long-term plan for the environment."[216]

Whereas the border communities were for the most part enthusiastic about the economic prospects raised by further trade and investment liberalization in Mexico, a loose coalition of environmental, labor, and consumer groups was generally skeptical about the benefits of free trade. For these groups the border, with its immense environmental and public health problems, represented a worst-case scenario of what a free trade agreement without adequate controls could mean for all of North America. After all, they rightly pointed out, the maquila sector has enjoyed liberalized trade and investment regulations for more than a quarter-century and look what havoc it has wreaked. Looking at the past record, many environmental organizations viewed the proposed free trade agreement with great skepticism. The environmental nightmare already seen on the border would be repeated throughout Mexico, they asserted, if proper guarantees were not inserted into the NAFTA treaty.

A couple of years before the NAFTA proposal was announced, national environmental groups such as the Environmental Defense Fund and the Sierra Club began to realize that international trade and investment were environmental issues. Environmental organizations had long been sponsoring conservation efforts abroad, such as the creation of nature reserves. Not until the late 1980s, however, did it become obvious that to protect the global environment, they would have to jump into the fray over the direction of global economics.

Free trade suddenly became a defining issue for the environmental movement. Washington's assurances that environmental issues would be adequately addressed in free trade negotiations with Mexico persuaded several organizations, including the Natural Resources Defense Council and World Wildlife Fund, to lend their support to congressional approval of a "fast track" for the trade negotiations. The inclusion of environmental provisions in the proposed accord signed in October 1992 was hailed as a victory by the Environmental Defense Fund, although other groups such as the Sierra Club and Friends of the Earth were more skeptical. More regionally based environmental organizations such as the Border Ecology Project, Texas Center for Policy Studies, and Arizona Toxics Information based their challenges to Washington's free trade proposals on their own experience with cross-border environmental problems.

The labor movement, consumer groups like Citizen Watch, and the left-of-center political sector also raised the environmental banner as part of their overall campaign to turn free trade into "fair trade." Although no firm political coalition was established, this rallying around the common denominator of the environment did help break down the narrow focus of the different special-interest groups. The labor movement moved beyond its strict economistic focus to consider the interface between environmental protection and occupational health. Through their association with unionists and progressive consumer organizations, some environmentalists broadened their definition of sustainable development to include more class-oriented issues such as worker safety and the basic right to a decent wage and affordable housing. Just as important, U.S. groups began to work and strategize with Mexican activists, broadening the point of view on each side of the border.

The U.S. government responded to this surge of activism in several ways—working with Mexico on the border plan, drafting the Environmental Review, and negotiating a side agreement to NAFTA to deal with environmental concerns, for instance. But it also moved to co-opt critics of NAFTA by creating a set of advisory bodies to channel public participation and siphon off opposition to the accord.[217] Invited to participate on these bodies were representatives of sectors like organized labor and the environmental movement. Keeping these groups on board or at least appearing to give their views careful consideration was critical to government strategies to obtain smooth acceptance of the trade agreement.

But the way these bodies were structured diluted the input of critics and beefed up the position of government and industry free traders. When NAFTA was being negotiated, for example, the Office of the U.S. Trade Representative set up a number of policy advisory committees that were supposed to channel recommendations from selected private sector representatives to NAFTA negotiators. Big business held the largest number of positions on these committees, outnumbering environmentalists by about thirty to one on the few committees that included representatives of environmental interest groups. Organized labor was similarly outnumbered, while groups seeking tough mandatory labor and environmental protections were not represented at all.

Participation was restricted in other ways as well. Although environmentalists won token positions on the services, agriculture, industry, and investment committees, the Bush administration refused to add an environmental committee to advise the Office of the U.S. Trade Representative on the trade agreement. Nor did the administration appoint environmentalists to committees advising on other areas with environmental impacts such as energy or the auto sector.

As NAFTA steamed ahead, the U.S. and Mexican governments also created public advisory committees (PACs) to keep border activists and environmentalists hooked into the IBEP and on board with the trade agreement. They are parallel bodies, one set up along the border in Mexico and one in the United States, to advise the EPA and SEDESOL and to funnel information to local communities.[218] In general terms, the appointed committees could play a useful role in helping to keep important border environmental issues on the table at the EPA and SEDESOL. But the Mexican government never appointed members to its PAC. In the United States, the committees have no actual authority, but they permit some needed public input into government border initiatives.

Winning hearts and minds along the border seems to be the major aim of the Foundation for Border Progress, a new binational grant-making organization launched with $50,000 seed money from the EPA.[219] Known in Mexico as the Fundación Progreso Fronterizo, the foundation was established to act as a matchmaker between community organizations that need resources and corporations, charitable groups, and government agencies with money to spend. It is intended to supplement the IBEP by pumping up self-help and volunteer efforts in health, environment, and social programs. By providing an easy way for businesses to chip into border improvement efforts—without being required to do so through increased taxes or similar mechanisms—the foundation may help popularize free trade, pacify activists, and do a public-relations favor for area businesses at one and the same time.

While activists from San Diego to Matamoros were trashing the draft IBEP, Richard Kiy, then EPA's border coordinator, and Timothy Atkeson, director of the EPA's international affairs office, hatched the idea for the foundation. Kiy has strong border business ties himself. He worked closely with the maquiladoras before he joined the EPA and served as program director for the Border Trade Alliance.[220]

Governed by a binational board of trustees, with top executive positions and staff split between the United States and Mexico, the foundation appears to be a true U.S.-Mexico initiative. Despite its binational structure, however, the Mexican component exists primarily on paper, and the U.S. government is the main spigot for donations to the foundation. The EPA will provide funds for both administration and grants. But SEDESOL, the agency in Mexico responsible for environmental affairs, has not yet said if it will contribute to the organization, and money from corporations has only begun to flow.

Most border groups are adopting a wait-and-see attitude toward the foundation. Along with many representatives of business interests, respected environmentalists and public health workers sit on the board, and a well-managed grant program could inject critically needed resources into deserving border organizations. But the foundation's government ties raise concerns that its creation was no more than a cynical political move to throw a few bones to environmental and community activists.

These government attempts to enlist activist and community organizations as allies on border programs reflect some gains for those concerned about environmental degradation. At least their views are being considered to some extent. But neither the United States nor Mexico has opened up the planning process to include the full participation of environmental and public health experts. And where they have been included—on the PACs, for instance—their perspectives are diluted by the views of others who wish to push full steam ahead on economic programs that are likely to exacerbate environmental conditions.

Moreover, the three NAFTA partners—the United States, Mexico, and Canada—announced in August 1993 the creation of a trilateral commission to resolve environmental disputes related to free trade. But the three governments do not plan to include citizen representatives on this important body. Instead the Commission on Environmental Cooperation will consist of government representatives, assisted by a panel of "experts" on trade and the environment but without defined avenues for citizen input. The provision for creating the commission was included in the Agreement on Environmental Cooperation, constructed as a supplemental agreement to NAFTA. Establishing such a body is a step forward in terms of international environmental protection in North America because it provides a forum to discuss problems, resolve disputes, and apply sanctions. But the commission's mandate will be restricted to problems of pollution prevention and wildlife preservation and will not extend to issues such as production processes, occupational health, or natural resource management. Along with few options for the participation of concerned citizens, these restrictions on the commission's scope of authority limit the usefulness of the body.

In response, environmental activists critical of the pact have called for the creation of a binational commission to focus not only on environmental concerns but also on health and labor issues generated by increasing integration between the United States and Mexico. They have urged that representatives of nongovernmental organizations and local government agencies with no vested interest in trade sit on the commission, along with representatives selected by the federal governments. And they have called for this proposed body to have the right to raise funds and allocate them for projects selected by the participants that will advance health and environment concerns and assure sustainable development as U.S.-Mexico economic integration goes forward.[221]

Chapter 5

Free Trade, the Environment, and the Consumer

Efforts to protect health and environment have in recent years clashed with the free trade agenda. On a global level, these conflicts have increasingly occurred within GATT and have come under consideration for the first time by the Organization for Economic Cooperation and Development (OECD) and the United Nations Conference on Environment and Development (UNCED). On a regional level, the tension between free trade principles and regulations safeguarding the environment and consumers has surfaced within the European Community and as part of the NAFTA negotiating process.

Environmentalists and consumer advocates have been pushing since the 1970s for international agreements and standards on such matters as endangered species protection, deforestation, and ozone control.[222] But it was not until 1990 that these groups made strong demands that the links between international trade and environmental and consumer issues be directly addressed as part of global and regional trade negotiations.

For too long environmental and safety concerns have been considered merely obstacles to the free flow of goods, services, and investment. At the heart of the environment and trade debate are national or local regulations that protect the environment or consumer safety but also function as nontariff trade barriers. Issues of sovereignty and extraterritoriality also arise in the intensifying debate about the place of environmental and consumer issues in free trade negotiations. Unrestricted free trade would abnegate a nation's ability to manage and conserve its own resources. Nations that adopt measures to preserve the family farm or to control the sale of timber, for example, could be faulted for resorting to unfair trade practices. Free trade agreements could also be used to block trade from nations with production processes that are harmful either to the environment or workers, such as drift-net fishing or the widespread use of child labor. In this sense, a lack of environmental regulations or insufficient enforcement of such regulations by exporting countries could be considered hidden trade subsidies.

Another contentious issue that must be resolved in free trade talks is the role of international standards for consumer products and the environment. It might seem that international standards set by the United Nations or some other global forum would be the ideal solution to resolve differences between trading nations. But although such international standards may represent an upward harmonization for less developed nations, they frequently represent a downward harmonization for industrialized countries with more advanced consumer and environmental regulations.

During 1990, as the Uruguay Round of the GATT entered what was expected to be its final year, these and other environmental/consumer concerns were raised for the first time.[223] In 1971 GATT had established a Group on Environmental Measures and International Trade, but it was not until 1991 that the rules committee was convened.[224] When the United States entered into free trade negotiations with Canada in 1986, the major U.S. environmental and consumer organizers showed little interest. The NAFTA negotiations, however, created great concern that regional integration under the banner of free trade was directly threatening the viability of U.S. environmental and health standards.

For many within the environmental community, alarm bells began ringing in early 1991 when a GATT dispute panel ruled in favor of a Mexican complaint that the United States could not fairly ban the importation of Mexican tuna. The United States, acting on the provisions of the Marine Mammal Protection Act, had prohibited the purchase of Mexican tuna on the grounds that Mexican tuna-fishing methods were killing substantial numbers of dolphins.[225] Environmentalists also became alarmed by new reports about environmental degradation along the U.S.-Mexico border. The fact that industries had begun using the 1988 U.S.-Canada Free Trade Treaty to challenge environmental standards and programs in both countries also increased environmental and consumer interest in international trade negotiations.

Recognizing that free trade talks represented the largest and most immediate threat to national and global efforts to protect the environment and citizen welfare, such groups as the Natural Resources Defense Council, Sierra Club, and Public Citizen dramatically increased their attention to international trade issues. Fair trade suddenly became the rallying call not only for labor and leftists who had long been questioning the direction of economic globalization but also for environmentalists and consumer advocates.

Environmentalist pressure did succeed in forcing GATT to consider the trade and environment connection for the first time, but it never became an integral issue within the Uruguay Round. With NAFTA the environmental community was more successful. Trade's impact on the environment and to a lesser degree on consumer health and safety became a prominent issue in the NAFTA debate. The relegation of environment to a "parallel track" in the negotiations frustrated environmentalists.[226] But because of their continuing pressure, the final NAFTA draft proved to be an improvement over the 1991 draft of the Uruguay Round (known as the Dunkel Draft), which had come under sharp criticism from environmental and consumer organizations.

The trade treaty signed in December 1992 was, according to Bush administration officials, "the greenest trade treaty ever." Most critics of the free trade proposal acknowledged the truth of that assessment, but noted that previous trade agreements had virtually ignored environmental concerns. In response to concerns raised by environmental and consumer organizations, NAFTA contained provisions that reduced the threat that domestic health and environmental standards would be automatically challenged as constituting nontariff barriers. Standards set by local, state, or national governments could be challenged only if they were designed primarily to block trade.

Rather than define consumer and environmental regulations as trade barriers, the agreement specified that such regulations would not be considered unnecessary barriers to trade if they have a legitimate objective and do not discriminate against particular countries. Among the legitimate objectives specified in the 1992 NAFTA proposal were measures to promote the interests of safety; human, animal, and plant life and health; environment; consumers; and sustainable development. However, the pact limits each party's protection of human, animal, and plant life to that within its own boundaries. A Canadian law intended to conserve Mexico's biodiversity would thus appear to be illegitimate under NAFTA.

Without requiring upward harmonization of standards, as many environmentalists and citizen groups had been advocating, the agreement stated that free trade should occur without curtailing environmental and consumer safeguards even if they were stricter in one country than another. In an important departure from GATT, where the burden of proof in disputes over nontariff barriers lies with the defending nation, the proposed NAFTA stated that the party challenging an environmental or consumer measure would have to prove that the defending country's regulation is inconsistent with the agreement.

Two other areas where the final draft showed improvement over earlier drafts concerned scientific justification and risk assessment of environmental and consumer measures. Although still ambiguous, the 1992 agreement appeared only to require that some scientific basis exist to support the formulation of these measures. Rather than insisting on risk/benefit analysis to justify environmental and consumer trade restrictions, the agreement instead stated that these measures be based on risk assessment and merely specified that each party "should take into account the objective of minimizing negative trade effects" in establishing food safety levels. Risk assessment is defined simply as an evaluation of potentially adverse effects rather than a judgment that would also consider the economic costs and benefits of these measures. Measures specifying "zero tolerance" for carcinogens would probably meet the obligation for risk assessment but might not be considered valid when employing risk/benefit analysis.[227]

In late 1993 the trinational Agreement on Environmental Cooperation, signed as a supplemental accord to NAFTA, brought many of the major U.S. environmental organizations on board in favor of NAFTA. These included the National Wildlife Federation, Conservation International, Natural Resources Defense Council, World Wildlife Fund, National Audubon Society, and Environmental Defense Fund. These environmental groups supported NAFTA not only because of new governmental commitments to pollution prevention, but also because they believed that NAFTA would open new channels of communication with Mexico over natural resources conservation and environmental protection. In her public endorsement of NAFTA, Kathryn Fuller, president of the World Wildlife Fund, noted that Mexico has more biological resources than almost any other country and that by acquiring greater economic opportunity through the trade agreement, Mexico would have more money available to protect the environment.

Although gratified that their lobbying and organizing had some success, many environmentalists remained critical of NAFTA as a model for international trade. One objection focused on the accord's failure to promote sustainable development, a concept whose goals include natural resource conservation, biological and cultural diversity, and equity. Although NAFTA listed the promotion of sustainable development as one of its objectives and defined it as a legitimate purpose for environmental regulations, it did not explicitly link trade and the environment—a link environmentalists argue is crucial to achieving sustainable development. An increasingly influential sector of the environmental movement also questions what free trade advocates assume—namely that economic growth is necessarily positive. It instead points to the environmentally destructive, exploitative, and inequitable character of what is commonly considered economic progress.

The continuing skepticism about global free trade proposals shared by many environmental and consumer organizations—and their opposition specifically to NAFTA—were based on more nuts-and-bolts considerations as well. These include the lack of funding and oversight to ensure that environmental regulations are enforced; the absence of public participation; the lack of rules governing production processes; sovereignty issues; and the lack of clear language defending the rights of communities and nations to set nondiscriminatory health, safety, and environmental regulations.

A common complaint among critics of NAFTA and GATT is that international trade regulations override democratic processes. Not only do the negotiations themselves take place behind closed doors with little opportunity for participation by citizens and nongovernmental organizations, but the dispute process for settling conflicts between trading parties is completely closed to citizen involvement and review. Only the executive branch of each party is empowered to bring a complaint to the Free Trade Commission that NAFTA would set up to resolve disputes. Individuals, unions, environmental groups, and local and state governments would need to persuade their country's president or prime minister to make their case for them under NAFTA. All arguments and documents presented to the commission would remain secret until fifteen days after the commission made its decision, and if the parties agreed not to

publish a final report of a given decision, the evidence and reasoning behind that decision would remain under wraps.[228]

Compounding this problem of the lack of citizen scrutiny and
participation is the undue influence exercised by major corporate
interests in the negotiating process. Not only are corporate representatives asked to participate in government working committees
on international trade, but these same interests are also generally
the ones who help write international standards for pesticide use,
food safety, and consumer products.[229]

For both environmental and consumer groups, right-to-know
provisions should also be incorporated into free trade agreements.
International product-labeling requirements would give consumers information about the substances and technologies used in
making imported goods, while workers would have access to similar information under right-to-know principles.

Closed dispute procedures, ambiguous language, and the lack
of strong guarantees in NAFTA left open the possibility that environmental and consumer protection regulations would not be in-
sulated from trade-motivated challenges. Environmental and
consumer groups want better guarantees that local, state, and
national standards will be respected. In this regard, they say that
government regulations that protect consumers and the environment should not be open to challenge simply because they are
higher than the international standard. Similarly, they argue that
international standards should be considered mainly a regulation
floor rather than a ceiling. Simply because a product is acceptable
by the international standard does not mean that the affected government should not follow its own review and approval procedures
for new products.

One of the key trade issues for environmentalists and consumer advocates is the need to apply standards to production
processes as well as to products themselves. Such standards
would protect the regional environment and cut down on destructive competition by ensuring that imports are not produced in a
manner that would violate environmental or health laws in the
importing country. NAFTA fails to distinguish itself from GATT in
this regard, a fact that worries environmentalists. They looked, for
example, for NAFTA expressly to reject GATT's interpretation of
the rules regarding the tuna and dolphin dispute, thus making

room for unilateral environmental measures that have an extra-territorial effect.

Environmentalists share labor activists' fear that even if free trade agreements protect local regulations, higher standards will be undermined as investment and jobs flow to countries with lower standards. Free trade agreements, they argue, must go further to facilitate the upward harmonization of health and environmental regulations to ensure that pollution-haven investment does not result. In this regard, funding mechanisms are essential to guarantee that countries like Mexico have the capacity to enforce their environmental laws. Furthermore, they say, lack of enforcement of such laws should constitute an unfair trade practice.

The fear that U.S. investment will seek pollution havens in Mexico stems from the basic disparities in environmental laws and enforcement between the United States and Mexico. But free traders argue that more integrated regional and global markets will promote economic growth. With this growth will come expanded environmental consciousness among a broadening Mexican middle class and increased revenues to support strong environmental programs. Most environmental organizations reject such reasoning, charging instead that economic growth inevitably means increased resource depletion and pollution without necessarily leading to tougher environmental regulation. In the best of circumstances, free trade without proper safeguards, funding, and guidelines may generate short-term economic gain for both trading partners but will not result in long-term or sustainable growth, according to environmental critics.[230]

Sovereignty, Internationalism, and Protectionism

Sovereignty and internationalism are two concepts that environmentalists and consumer advocates are struggling to reconcile. It is commonly agreed that the sovereign right of nations to protect their citizenry, conserve their environments, and uphold social values must be recognized in free trade agreements. But at the same time certain international rules and norms are clearly needed to protect the global environment and to regulate what is increasingly a global economy. To make such global standards meaningful, nations must cede some of their sovereignty.

Generally the more industrialized nations would benefit from an upward harmonization of environmental and health standards. As all standards improved, less developed countries would be less able to use lower standards as a type of indirect subsidy to their exporting industries, and corporations from the more developed nations would have less incentive to relocate. But countries like Mexico could rightly charge that their sovereignty would be undermined if they were forced to abide by the regulations established by more developed and wealthier nations. Reacting to demands by environmentalists and consumer advocates for phased-in upward harmonization, a spokesperson for the Bush Department of State accused U.S. environmentalists of being "latter-day colonialists" and said that such proposals were simply a "new justification for keeping the Latins down."[231]

Sovereignty also becomes an issue with recent proposals to regulate the foreign operations of U.S. corporations and to create increased access for foreign citizens with complaints against U.S. investors or products. One such proposal is for a U.S. Foreign Environmental Practices Act, modeled after the Foreign Corrupt Practices Act, which would make U.S. citizens and corporations subject to both criminal and civil prosecution in U.S. courts for violating applicable U.S. environmental law. Such a law would probably go a long way toward persuading U.S. corporations investing in Mexico to improve their environmental practices. Its supporters say that it would also increase corporate accountability by making firms more responsible to consumers, workers, and the communities in which they invest. Given the fact that Mexican courts will not consider suits against corporations for violating environmental laws, this proposal has gained support among many Mexican as well as U.S. environmentalists. But for other Mexicans such proposals revive fears of Yankee domination. Mexican problems should be resolved by Mexicans, they say.[232]

In relation to free trade, the sovereignty debate also extends to such issues as saving the family farm, protecting small businesses, restricting the exploitation of natural resources, and fostering certain industries as part of a national development policy. Questions of sovereignty also come into play when considering if free trade agreements should contain clauses requiring respect for basic human, labor, and political rights.

If free trade is to be more than a corporate bill of rights, such issues need to be considered in establishing rules for global and regional integration. Strong and enforceable norms for basic human rights are essential to guarantee that countries do not achieve unfair trade advantages because their workers are repressed and exploited. Such standards already exist in the United Nations' International Labor Organization and the Universal Declaration of Human Rights.[233]

Linking free trade agreements to this kind of internationalism would help ensure a "level playing field" for trade. Arguments about national sovereignty represent the worst kind of protectionism when they defend a country's failure to meet international standards for human rights, labor organizing, and political freedom. But a new world order cannot and should not mean one in which communities and nations no longer have the right to protect their own social or cultural values or to set their own development policies.

The ideal of free trade and global integration must make room for such protections if economies are to grow and societies are to prosper. Even if some economic inefficiencies and trade barriers are involved, free trade agreements should allow for measures that save family farms, sustain local cultures, or protect other important social values of trade partners. Similarly, community and national economic development goals—such as food security, agrarian reform programs, or industrial development policies—cannot be ignored simply to make it easier for transnational investors and traders to conduct their business.

Some of the harshest criticism of NAFTA and U.S. free trade initiatives has come from Ralph Nader's consumer watchdog group Public Citizen. Nader has accused GATT of "imposing a mega-corporate view of the world." Staff attorney Lori Wallach charged that the revisions reflected in the final NAFTA draft were merely cosmetic and that the two side agreements reached in 1993 did not do nearly enough to outweigh the overall negative impact of the proposed agreement. According to Wallach, "The United States and other nations are at a crossroads. The rapidly expanding global marketplace threatens to overwhelm citizens' ability to exercise democratic sovereignty by legislating rules that will govern their societies. Multinational corporations want global commerce but without corresponding global law to hold them accountable."[234]

Sustainable Development

Sustainable development has become a key term in the debate over economic integration and the joint future of Mexico and the United States. Although the term has been appropriated by free trade proponents as part of their attempt to persuade the public that international agreements such as the GATT and NAFTA will actually benefit the environment, sustainable development is a more radical concept when used by many environmental activists. Simply defined, it signifies a type of economic development that attempts to meet the needs of the present generation without compromising the needs of future generations.[235] Recognizing the finite quantity of natural resources, sustainable development implies an environmental stewardship of the planet and accepts the natural limits of economic growth. Put in economic terms, sustainability means living off nature's "income" while not dissipating its "capital"—that is, limiting consumption to the amount that can be sustained indefinitely without degrading the environmental resources that constitute capital stocks.[236]

This environmentally based concept of development contrasts sharply with those wedded to the trickle-down theory of economic and human progress. This approach casts economic growth in entirely positive terms. As the argument goes, only through economic growth will communities have the resources to devote to environmental protection. As stated by the rightist Heritage Foundation, "Growth is more conducive to a clean environment than stagnation."[237] In this view, there is little room in either the free market or free trade to consider such "externalities" as the social and environmental costs of economic growth. Rather, as the economy grows, so will its capacity—and the willingness of the society—to resolve these resultant problems. Rephrasing this philosophy, Michael Gregory of Arizona Toxics Information remarked, "The pro-trade argument that developing nations will be able to clean up and protect the environment when they get rich from free trade might be more accurately stated as *if* they get rich from free trade, they *may* try to clean up the pollution caused by getting rich."[238]

In their efforts to include environmental provisions in such trade agreements as the GATT and NAFTA, environmental organizations want to distinguish themselves from the nationalists and protectionists who also oppose unregulated free trade. Most environmentalists have no argument against removing tariff and nontariff barriers erected solely for the protection of different economic sectors. But there is a belief that individual nations should retain the ability to block trade and investment that contravenes sustainable development principles. The three main concerns in this regard are that international accords will preempt local environmental regulations, will tend to harmonize environmental standards downward, and will prohibit restrictions on resource exploitation such as the right of a country to restrict the rate of timber harvesting or oil extraction. Closely related to this last concern is the issue of whether a country has the right to prohibit the importation of certain goods for strictly environmental reasons, such as outlawing the purchase of tropical timber as a way to protect the world's rapidly diminishing rainforests.

Environmentalists committed to sustainable development principles are concerned that free trade will limit the ability of nations to use tariff and nontariff barriers as part of sustainable development strategies that protect open space and family farms. And they object to narrow environmental standards based on cost-benefit analysis, particularly if the costs are being analyzed by those who have no commitment to resource conservation and sustainable development. In such an analysis, they ask how will such intangible costs as the losing of a wilderness, the undermining of the quality of life, or the extinction of another species be measured? Moreover, they argue that the standards and safeguards set in place by local communities, states, or national governments regarding health, safety, and the environment should not be open to challenge through free trade accords—even if these measures are open to scientific debate or are not based on strict cost-benefit analysis.

Yet more than a movement of naysayers, the environmentalists who have raised objections to free trade have also proposed reforms that they contend would reduce the environmental repercussions of free trade and economic development. In contrast with the secrecy cherished by trade diplomats, they want trade negotiations to be open to public participation, and they demand that right-to-know principles for workers and affected communities be a condition for all transborder investment. Concerns about runaway plants would diminish, they contend, if corporations were prevented from using double standards for labor and the environment at home and abroad. Some of the suggested measures, such as imposing countervailing tariffs on polluting industries, run di rectly against the principles of free trade. Other suggestions, such as allowing foreigners to sue U.S. corporations in U.S. courts or insisting that trading partners abide by U.S. environmental standards, would allow more public control of transnational corporations but raise other nationalist concerns about extraterritorial sovereignty.[239]

At the same time that environmental organizations have been fighting to see that more "green language" be inserted into international trade accords, many of them have also been mobilizing citizen environmental activism across international boundaries. They recognize that the most effective way to prevent pollution havens and to protect international ecosystems is to work more closely with local groups in Mexico. These groups can then put direct pressure on their own governments and on corporations in their communities to ensure that appropriate environmental and health safeguards are respected. Such organizations as the Pesticide Action Network and Health Action International have demonstrated the effectiveness of coordinated international campaigns in raising consumer and official awareness about the global marketing of harmful substances. Especially along the border, U.S.-Mexico coalitions of environmental and community groups are also slowly emerging. In Mexico such new organizations as the Committee for Ecological Disclosure in Mexicali and Green Border Tijuana serve as models for new citizen activism around environmental and health concerns.

In Mexico, as in the United States, environmentalism is gaining new political and economic dimensions. Demands for corporate responsibility, environmental and occupational health guarantees, and public disclosure about hazardous wastes raise questions about the lack of democracy and the inequitable development patterns in Mexico. Similarly, environmentalists in the United States have found that demands for the inclusion of environmental protection measures in trade agreements rightly cannot be made without also considering such related issues as occupational safety and the living conditions of Mexican workers at U.S.-owned plants. In both countries the call for sustainable development has highlighted the deficiencies associated with current economic policy making while pointing out the need for national development strategies that both protect the environment and meet basic human needs.

References

1. Some 200 Mexicans, including Sotelo, received among the largest doses of radiation on record for the public. Susan West, "Hot," *Science*, Dec. 1984.

2. In terms of the number of exposed people, the Juárez incident falls between the Chernobyl and Three Mile Island catastrophes, according to sources cited in Paul Salopek's excellent investigative report, "Global Trade in Used Technology Imperils the Unwary," *El Paso Times*, 28 July 1991. The following description relies largely on this report, Katherine Silberger's "¡Desastre!" *Village Voice*, 16 June 1992, and West's "Hot" (ibid.). Also see Eliot Marshall, "Juárez: An Unprecedented Radiation Accident," *Science*, March 1984, 1152-54, and *Contaminated Mexican Steel Incident* (Washington, DC: U.S. Nuclear Regulatory Commission, 1985).

3. The importation of the radiotherapy machine by the Juárez doctor did, however, violate Mexican government regulations. By law, importers of such equipment are required to notify the National Commission on Nuclear Safety and Safeguards (CONSENUSA), which has the authority to regulate the import, export, transport, operation, and maintenance of nuclear devices.

4. *World Bank Staff Appraisal*, 1000-5 ME, 19 March 1992.

5. For a good overview of environmental problems outside the border, see *Environmental and Health Issues in the Interior of Mexico: Options for Transnational Safeguards* (Bisbee, AZ: Border Ecology Project and Proyecto Fronterizo de Educación Ambiental, 1993).

6. For more on the environmental implications of a trade-based food policy in Mexico see Steven E. Sanderson, "Mexico's Environmental Future," *Current History* 92, no. 571 (Feb. 1993).

7. See Hilary F. French, "Costly Tradeoffs: Reconciling Trade and the Environment," *Worldwatch Paper* 113, March 1993.

8. Ibid.

9. Alvar W. Carlson, "Geography and Environment," in Ellwyn R. Stoddard, Richard L. Nostrand, and Jonathan P. West, *Borderlands Sourcebook: A Guide to the Literature on Northern Mexico and the American Southwest* (Norman: University of Oklahoma Press, 1983), 75-80.

10. Leon C. Metz, *Border: The U.S.-Mexico Line* (El Paso: Mangan Books, 1990), 293.

11. Jim Carrier, "The Colorado: A River Drained Dry," *National Geographic*, June 1991, 4. Also see Todd Sargent, "Wildlife Hangs in the Balance as Wetlands Studies Commence," *Transboundary Resources Report*, Summer 1993.

12. For more on this viewpoint see Francisco A. Malagamba, "Troublesome Equity in the Distribution of Shared Water Resources: The U.S.-Mexico Border," in Paul Ganster and Hartmut Walter, eds., *Environmental Hazards and Bioresource Management in the United States-Mexico Borderlands* (Los Angeles: UCLA Latin American Center Publications, 1990), 13-21.

13. The IBWC was established in 1932 as the merger of two binational agencies—the International Boundary Commission (created in 1889 to manage disputes along the international boundary) and the International Water Commission, a less important agency established in the 1920s. An overview of the functioning of the IBWC and an examination of how the U.S. and Mexican counterparts differ is found in Stephen P. Mumme, "Engineering Diplomacy: The Evolving Role of the International Boundary and Water Commission in U.S.-Mexico Water Management," *Journal of Borderlands Studies* 1, no. 1 (Spring 1986):74-108.

14. A drought in the 1870s resulted in water shortages along the Rio Grande, and the Mexican government accused Colorado and New Mexico of stealing water. It charged that increased water use by those states was causing Mexicans to suffer water shortages. In 1895 U.S. Attorney General Judson Harmon disputed Mexico's claim, asserting that the United States enjoyed "absolute sovereignty" over the Rio Grande. According to Francisco A. Malagamba, "Mexican agricultural producers have consistently maintained their disagreement with regard to their international rights to the waters of the Rio Bravo" since the turn of the century. For more on Mexico's view of water use along the border, see Malagamba, "Troublesome Equity," in Ganster and Walter, *Environmental Hazards and Bioresource Management*, 13-21 (n. 12).

15. The upper basin states are Utah, Wyoming, Colorado, New Mexico, and northern Arizona, while the lower basin states are California, Nevada, and southern Arizona.

16. Anne M. Morgan, "Transboundary Liability Goes with the Flow? Gasser v. United States: The Use and Misuse of a Treaty," *Transboundary Resources Report*, Summer 1991, 1. Furthermore, in a time of extreme drought the river flow may drop as low as 6 maf, and conversely in an extremely wet period rise to 25 maf.

17. The 1944 Treaty Relating to the Utilization of Waters of the Colorado and Tijuana Rivers and of the Rio Grande established the framework to apportion the waters of all ephemeral and nonephemeral streams and rivers—not just the Rio Grande and the Colorado River—crossing the land boundary. The rights of the two countries with respect to this other surface water have never been fully defined, however. The standard source on international negotiations regarding the distribution of these two rivers is Norris Hundley Jr., *Dividing the Waters: A Century of Controversy between the United States and Mexico* (Berkeley: University of California Press, 1966).

18. Albert E. Utton, "Transboundary Water Quality: Institutional Alternatives," in Ganster and Walter, *Environmental Hazards and Bioresource Management*, 49.

19. See Francisco Oyarzabel-Tamargo, *Economic Impact of Saline Irrigation Water: Mexicali Valley, Mexico* (Ann Arbor: University of Michigan Press, 1976).

20. It was agreed that the salinity of the water passed on to Mexico must be within 145 ppm of that found at Imperial Dam.

21. Jennifer Warren, "Yuma Desalination Plant Comes of Age—Too Late," *Los Angeles Times*, 8 March 1992.

22. For a revealing look at the uneconomic character of the Yuma plant, see Allen Kneese, "Environmental Stress and Political Conflicts: Salinity in the Colorado River," *Transboundary Resources Report*, Summer 1990.

23. The power of western agribusiness, its dependence on government subsidies, and the generally wasteful use of limited water in the West is clearly demonstrated by Marc Reisner, *Cadillac Desert: The American West and Its Disappearing Water* (New York: Viking, 1986).

24. Gail Sevrens, *Environment, Health, and Housing Needs and Nonprofit Groups in the U.S.-Mexico Border Area* (Arlington, VA: World Environment Center, 1992), 55. This is a valuable overview of environmental health problems and issues, as well as a comprehensive directory of nongovernmental organizations concerned with these issues.

25. Salinity over 700 ppm begins to cause crop damage, while 500 ppm is the upper limit for potable water. See Kneese, "Environmental Stress," 1 (n. 22).

26. Warren, "Yuma Desalination Plant" (see n. 21).

27. Interview with Jesús Román Calleros, Colegio de la Frontera Norte, Mexicali, 2 May 1991.

28. Testimony by John Hall, chair of the Texas Water Commission, to the EPA, 20 Sept. 1991.

29. Raul Fernandez, "The Economic Evolution of the Imperial (U.S.A.) and Mexicali (Mexico) Valleys," *Journal of Borderlands Studies* 6, no. 2 (Fall 1991):10, 11.

30. Mexico claims that lining the canal violates Minute 242 of the 1973 agreement that provides for mutual consultation before the undertaking of new developments affecting either surface or groundwaters or of any substantial modifications of present facilities. But the United States responds that the minute requires only consultation, not consent. Furthermore, it asserts that Mexico is regularly receiving its 1.5 maf of Colorado River water and has no claim on additional water. Mexico contends that the United States never objected to its capturing of All-American Canal seepage—which it has been doing since the 1950s—and that the United States cannot now try to capture conserved waters (meaning waters gained by human initiatives such as dams or vegetation removal projects), a position amply supported by U.S. water rights law. Possible solutions to this problem include pumping a portion of the conserved waters to Mexico or providing Tijuana with treated wastewaters from a planned treatment plant south of San Diego. In her examination of the conflict, Melissa Crane observed that the case pits future users of water (California cities buying the water from the Imperial Irrigation District) against the present agricultural, industrial, and domestic users in Baja California. She concluded that "the needs of future users need to be considered certainly, but it would seem less equitable to ruin a vibrant economy in one region than to prevent development in another." Melissa Crane, "Diminishing Water Resources and International Law: U.S.-Mexico, A Case Study," *Cornell International Law Journal* 24 (1991):318-19. Also see Douglas Hayes, "The All-American Canal Lining Project: A Catalyst for Rational and Comprehensive Groundwater Management on the United States-Mexico Border," and J. Román Calleros, "The Impact on Mexico of the Lining of the All-American Canal," *Natural Resources Journal* 31 (Fall 1991); and Albert E. Utton, "A Tale of Six Cities and the All-American Canal," *Transboundary Resources Report*, Summer 1990.

31. See Stephen P. Mumme, *Apportioning Groundwater Beneath the U.S.-Mexico Border* (San Diego: Center for U.S.-Mexican Studies, 1988).

32. See College of Engineering, University of Texas at El Paso, and Public Service Board, *Development and Water in El Paso/Juárez: Limited Resources for Growing Needs* (El Paso, April 1991).

33. John C. Day, "International Aquifer Management: The Hueco Bolson on the Rio Grande," *Natural Resources Journal* 18 (Jan. 1978):173.

34. There are, however, few international models for a groundwater treaty as explained in Crane, "Diminishing Water Resources," 299-323 (see n. 30). Not only is international law on groundwater nearly nonexistent, but any attempt to formulate a U.S.-Mexico treaty would have to confront the scientific uncertainty regarding the nature of groundwater, such as its sources and its quantity.

35. Crane, "Diminishing Water Resources," 319 (see n. 30).

36. The principle of prior appropriation which is applied throughout the West (except in Texas) stipulates that water is allocated on the basis of first use and that subsequent users will be apportioned amounts less than the first user.

37. C. Richard Bath and Dilmus D. James, "Transborder Flows of Technical Information: Cases of the Commercialization of Guayule and Groundwater Utilization," working

paper, U.S.-Mexico Project Series, no. 10 (Washington, DC: Overseas Development Council, July 1982), 13.

38. Albert Utton sees Texas as the primary obstacle to an international groundwater treaty, observing, "The political opposition in Texas is so strongly against regulation that the IBWC, which depends on the Texas congressional delegation for its support, has been unable to take a strong role." Cited in Jan Gilbreath Rich, "Bordering on Trouble," *Environmental Forum*, May-June 1991, 32.

39. See Albert E. Utton, "Anticipating Transboundary Resource Needs and Issues in the U.S.-Mexico Border Region," *Natural Resources Journal*, 22 Oct. 1982, 735-74.

40. The two Rio Grande basins are governed by separate international agreements. The Upper Rio Grande Basin, which carries the water south to Fort Quitman, Texas (east of El Paso), is regulated internationally by the U.S.-Mexico Treaty of 1906, which allocates 60,000 acre-feet to Mexico per year. The Lower Rio Grande Basin, extending from El Paso to the Gulf of Mexico, is governed by the 1944 Treaty Relating to the Utilization of Waters of the Colorado and Tijuana Rivers and of the Rio Grande, which divides the flow of the Rio Grande roughly equally between Texas and Mexico. For a brief overview of U.S.-Mexico water history and current issues, see Albert E. Utton, "The Importance of United States-Mexico Water Relations," in Zachary A. Smith, ed., *Water and the Future of the Southwest* (Albuquerque: University of New Mexico Press, 1989), 71-88. The best source on current management issues for the Rio Grande is David J. Easton and David Hurlbut, *Challenges in the Binational Management of Water Resources in the Rio Grande/Rio Bravo* (Austin: U.S.-Mexican Policy Studies Program, University of Texas at Austin, 1992).

41. Cited in *Life*, Nov. 1987.

42. According to the California Governor's Water Policy Task Force Report (1992), current overuse of groundwater reserves combined with reduced water availability from the Colorado River as Arizona takes its full legal entitlements will contribute to a yearly reduction of up to 2.5 maf of water from current levels. This is equivalent to the amount of water used each year by ten million families of four.

43. College of Engineering et al., *Development and Water*, 3 (see n. 32).

44. The Center for Environmental Resource Management (CERM) at the University of Texas at El Paso has guided the creation of the Binational Water Policy Institute. There are similar proposals for the creation of binational commissions to address the magnitude of environmental and public health problems along the border. Through the offices of the IBWC and the Pan American Health Organization, there have long been indirect channels of communication between border cities.

45. Mary E. Kelly et al., "U.S.-Mexico Free Trade Negotiations and the Environment," *Columbia Journal of World Business* (Summer 1991):51, citing Alberto Székely, legal adviser to the Mexican Foreign Ministry.

46. For an overview of the environmental crisis in Sonora, see José Luis Moreno, "El deterioro del medio ambiente," *Revista de El Colegio de Sonora* 2 (Jan. 1991).

47. For a loving description of the region by a naturalist who has traveled its extent, see Frederick Gehlbach, *Mountain Islands and Desert Streams: A Natural History of the U.S.-Mexican Borderlands* (College Station: Texas A&M Press, 1981).

48. Gary Paul Nabhan, "Desert Rescuers," *World Monitor* 36 (July 1992).

49. Salvador Contreras, *Peces en peligro de extinción: Agua y perspectivas de desarrollo en zonas aridas de México* (Austin: Texas Center for Policy Studies, 1991).

50. Steve LaRue, "Many Gulf of California Species 'in Agony,' " *San Diego Union-Tribune*, 25 July 1992.

51. Larry B. Stammer, "The Gulf of Mexico Besieged," *Los Angeles Times*, 15 June 1990. For a brief overview of environmental degradation of the Gulf of Mexico, also see *Integrated Environmental Plan for the Mexican-U.S. Border Area* (Washington, DC: En-

vironmental Protection Agency and Secretariat of Urban Development and Ecology, 1992), iii, 10-11. In response to increased contamination of the gulf, the EPA has established a multiagency Gulf of Mexico Program, whose director was cited by the *Los Angeles Times* as saying that the Gulf of Mexico is quickly approaching a point of irreversible environmental impacts.

52. Interview with Rose Farmer, 19 Aug. 1992.

53. Testimony by Gary Mauro to the EPA on 16 Sept. 1991 at McAllen, Texas.

54. William Branigin, "Mexico's Other Contraband—Wildlife," *Washington Post*, 24 June 1989, citing U.S. Fish and Wildlife Service Chief of Law Enforcement Jerome S. Smith.

55. Cited in Steve LaRue, "Profits Keep Bird Smugglers Coming North," *San Diego Union-Tribune*, 16 Sept. 1991.

56. Interview with Kris Sarri, Defenders of Wildlife, 16 July 1992.

57. For an excellent examination of these issues see Debra A. Rose, *A North American Free Trade Agreement: The Impacts on Wildlife Trade* (Washington, DC: World Wildlife Fund, 1991).

58. Branigin, "Mexico's Other Contraband—Wildlife" (see n. 54).

59. *World Bank Staff Appraisal* (see n. 4).

60. *Ecología Sonora*, no. 1 (Hermosillo: Movimiento Ecologista de Sonora, 1991).

61. Hartmut Walter, "Borderlands Bioresources: A Unique Scientific and Political Challenge," in Ganster and Walter, *Environmental Hazards and Bioresource Management*, 261-70 (see n. 12).

62. Interview with Dr. Laurance Nickey, 30 July 1992.

63. This crisis emerged in 1961 as a result of the U.S. water substitution from the Wellton-Mohawk irrigation district outside Yuma, Arizona.

64. For a good overview of U.S.-Mexico environmental concerns in the 1980s, see C. Richard Bath, "Environmental Issues in the United States-Mexico Borderlands," in Ina Rosenthal-Urey, ed., *Regional Impacts of U.S.-Mexican Relations* (San Diego: Center for U.S.-Mexican Studies, 1986), 50-72.

65. Interview with Jesús Reynoso, El Paso City–County air-quality official, 23 July 1992.

66. Mary Kelly, *Facing Reality: The Need for Fundamental Changes in Protecting the Environment along the U.S.-Mexico Border* (Austin: Texas Center for Policy Studies, Oct. 1991), 2.

67. Cited in Marjorie Miller, "S.D. Plan for Sewage Plant a Dead Issue," *Los Angeles Times*, 10 March 1984.

68. Interview with Nickey (see n. 62).

69. Ken Baake, "ASARCO Ranked in Nation's Worst Chemical Polluters," *El Paso Herald-Post*, 16 May 1990.

70. Recent renovations of the smelter have substantially reduced levels of these contaminants.

71. Until recently, this problem of contamination was heightened by the fact that in Nogales, Arizona, produce was sprayed regularly with water from wells contaminated by untreated sewage flowing north across the border.

72. "A Permanent U.S.-Mexico Border Environmental Health Commission," report by the Council on Scientific Affairs, *Journal of the American Medical Association* 263, no. 24 (27 June 1990):3320.

73. Bath, "Environmental Issues" (see n. 64).

74. Minute 261 concerning border sanitation problems was the immediate result of a joint declaration by presidents Carter and López Portillo calling upon the IBWC "to make immediate recommendations for faster progress toward a permanent solution to the sanitation of waters along the border." The key clause of the resolution provides that

the two governments recognize as a "border sanitation problem each case in which, in the judgment of the Commission, the waters that cross the border, including coastal water, or flow in the limitrophe reaches of the Rio Grande and the Colorado River, have sanitary conditions that present a hazard to the health and well-being of the inhabitants of either side of the border or impair the beneficial uses of these waters." This language is broad enough to offer the opportunity for the commission to expand its efforts beyond traditional sewage disposal works to cover the range of problems from salinity to toxic industrial and deleterious agricultural practices. See Utton, "Transboundary Water Quality," 55 (n. 18).

75. Stephen Mumme, "The Background and Significance of Minute 261 of the International Boundary and Water Commission," *California Western Law Journal* 2 (1981):223, 226. Mumme suggested that the commission "has interpreted its powers conservatively in such a manner as to preclude the possibility of any serious controversy over the propriety of its jurisdiction."

76. See, for example, Kelly, *Facing Reality*, 3 (n. 66). The environmental policy center at which Kelly works recommended the "removal of IBWC's lead jurisdiction on water quality problems in border area rivers and underground water and the transfer of that jurisdiction to a new binational agency that is open to public participation and accountable to border area governments."

77. Sevrens, *Environmental, Health, and Housing Needs*, 12 (see n. 24).

78. Cited in Greg Moran, "Tijuana Break Again Sends Sewage to U.S.," *San Diego Union-Tribune*, 8 Aug. 1992.

79. Cited in Kathryn Balint, "City Pressed on Border Sewage Pipe," *San Diego Union-Tribune*, 26 July 1992.

80. Seth Mydans, "U.S. and Mexico Agree on Border Sewage Plant," *New York Times*, 22 Aug. 1990.

81. José Luis Calderón, "Policies and Strategies for the Control of Contamination of Water on the Northern Mexican Border," in Ganster and Walter, *Environmental Hazards and Bioresource Management*, 38 (see n. 12).

82. Sevrens, *Environmental, Health, and Housing Needs*, 67 (see n. 24).

83. Edward Cody, "Expanding Waste Line Along Mexico's Border," *Washington Post*, 17 Feb. 1992.

84. James E. Garcia, "Border River Laden with Wastes," *Austin American-Statesman*, 29 Sept. 1991.

85. Cited in Nancy Cleeland, "A Border Boom Has Its Ugly Side, Too," *San Diego Union-Tribune*, 16 Feb. 1992.

86. Interview with Reynoso (see n. 65).

87. Bath, "Environmental Issues" (see n. 64).

88. Interview with Reynoso (see n. 65).

89. Cited in Sharon Spivik, "Tougher Smog Checks Urged for Commuters from Mexico," *San Diego Union-Tribune*, 29 April 1992.

90. Cited in Michael J. Kennedy, "On Texas Border: Outlook for Air Quality is Murky," *Los Angeles Times*, 20 Nov. 1991.

91. The Border Ecology Project and the Northeast Sonora–Cochise County Health Council have charged that the Compañia Mexicana de Cananea (majority ownership held by Mexican copper magnate Jorge Larrea with 22 percent ownership held by the U.S.-owned ASARCO) has expanded without meeting control standards specified under Annex 4 of the 1983 La Paz Agreement.

92. Cited in Kennedy, "On Texas Border" (see n. 90).

93. Statement of Dr. Laurance N. Nickey, joint hearing before the Committee on Environment and Public Works, 23 April 1991, 26.

94. *Health Care: Availability in the Texas-Border Area* (Washington, DC: General Accounting Office, Oct. 1988), 2.

95. Interview with Nickey (see n. 62).

96. Ricardo Loewe Reiss, "Considerations on the Health Status along Mexico's Northern Border," in Stanley R. Ross, ed., *Views across the Border: The United States and Mexico* (Albuquerque: University of New Mexico Press, 1978), 251.

97. Numerous works document the environmental and occupational health problems associated with the maquiladora industry. One of the most recent is "Overview of Environmental Issues Associated with Maquiladora Development along the Texas-Mexico Border" (Austin: Texas Center for Policy Studies, Oct. 1990).

98. Cited in James E. García, "Trade Casts Light on Environment," *Austin American-Statesman*, 30 Sept. 1991.

99. Jane Juffer, "The Case of the Mallory Children," *Progressive*, Oct. 1988, 27.

100. This is according to statistics for the 1980-88 period published by the International Register of Congenital Deformities. According to Rick Finell, a geneticist at Texas A&M University, Latinos are one of several populations, including the Welsh, Irish, and Chinese, that have shown susceptibility to the disorder. Cited in Ana Arana, "The Wasteland," *San Francisco Chronicle*, 30 Aug. 1991.

101. Coalition for Justice in the Maquiladoras, press release, 1 July 1992.

102. Cited in Gaynell Terrell, "Tragic Puzzle Grips Families on the Border," *Houston Post*, 19 May 1992.

103. Secretaría de Salud, Jurisdicción Sanitaria No. 2, "Protocolo de Investigación de Anencefalia 1989-92" (Ciudad Juárez, 1992).

104. Cited in Roberto Suro, "Pollution Tests Two Neighbors: El Paso and Juárez," *New York Times*, 23 Dec. 1991.

105. C. Richard Bath, "U.S.-Mexico Experience in Managing Transboundary Air Resources: Problems, Prospects, and Recommendations for the Future," in César Sepulveda and Albert Utton, eds., *The U.S.-Mexico Border Region: Anticipating Resource Needs and Issues to the Year 2000* (El Paso: Texas Western Press, 1982), 426.

106. Cited in Mydans, "U.S. and Mexico Agree" (see n. 80).

107. *Transboundary Resources Report*, Summer 1990, 4.

108. Cited in Paul Salopek, "Crowded Border Imports High Rates of Disease," *El Paso Times*, 14 May 1991.

109. Mark Dowie, "The Corporate Crime of the Century," *Mother Jones*, Nov. 1979, 23-49, and Thomas N. Gladwin, "Environment, Development, and Multinational Enterprise," in Charles S. Pearson, ed., *Multinational Corporations, Environment, and the Third World* (Durham: Duke University Press, 1987), 16.

110. See Susan Fletcher, "International Environmental Issues: Overview," *CRS Issue Brief* (Washington, DC: Congressional Research Service, 27 July 1992).

111. The term *circle of poison* was popularized by the publication of David Weir and Mark Shapiro, *The Circle of Poison* (San Francisco: Institute for Food and Development Policy, 1981).

112. According to a study by the Foundation for Advancements in Science and Education, every hour U.S. companies export more than four tons of pesticides banned, canceled, withdrawn, or restricted from the U.S. market. About a quarter of exported pesticides are not registered by the EPA for use in the United States. Foundation for Advancements in Science and Education, "Special Report: Exporting Banned and Hazardous Pesticides" (Los Angeles, 1991). According to the EPA, about half of Latin American pesticide imports come from the United States. *Food Safety and Quality: Five Countries' Efforts to Meet U.S. Requirements on Imported Produce* (Washington, DC: General Accounting Office, March 1990). Also see *Pesticides: Export of Unregistered Pesticides is*

Not Adequately Monitored by EPA (Washington, DC: General Accounting Office, April 1989).

113. *Pesticides: Better Sampling and Enforcement Needed on Imported Food* (Washington, DC: General Accounting Office, Sept. 1986), 3.

114. Interview with Jack Grady, El Paso, 24 July 1992.

115. Angus Wright, *The Death of Ramón González: The Modern Agricultural Dilemma* (Austin: University of Texas Press, 1990), 196, citing U.S. government surveys. This excellent book not only offers a compelling personal portrait of the occupational hazards of farmworkers in Mexico but is a persuasive argument for a radical reform of the agricultural economy in Mexico.

116. Ibid. and "Imported Produce," *Los Angeles Times*, 9 April 1989.

117. Cited in Michael Weisskopf, "Pesticide Safety Tests: Can They Be Trusted?" *Washington Post*, 13 March 1991.

118. Statement of William Ramsey of the Western Growers Association before the U.S. House of Representatives Committee on Agriculture, 24 April 1991.

119. DDT is "restricted" in Mexico and legally used only for the control of malaria and dengue vectors, although the organochlorine continues to be used clandestinely, especially in the more remote parts of the country.

120. *Food Safety and Quality*, Appendix V (see n. 112).

121. Angus Wright, "Third World Pesticide Production," *Global Pesticide Campaigner* 1, no. 3 (June 1991).

122. Angus Wright, "Rethinking the Circle of Poison: The Politics of Pesticide Poisoning Among Mexican Farm Workers," *Latin American Perspectives* 13, no. 4 (Fall 1986):30.

123. Marco Luis Patiño, "Agroquímico quema a jornaleros," *El Imparcial*, 7 Feb. 1991.

124. Wright, *The Death of Ramón González*, 41 (see n. 115).

125. Ibid., 12, citing a 1987 interview with a representative of Mexico's National Union of Vegetable Growers.

126. For the place of Mixtec labor in agricultural production, see Michael Kearney, "Integration of the Mixteca and the Western U.S.-Mexico Region via Migratory Wage Labor," in Rosenthal-Urey, *Regional Impacts*, 71-102 (n. 64).

127. Researchers at the Agricultural Research Station of the Northwest (CIANO), among others, have predicted this scenario. Rosenthal-Urey, *Regional Impacts*, 37 (see n. 64).

128. Sources on the economic viability of alternative and traditional farming methods include Jennifer Curtis, *Harvest of Hope: The Potential of Alternative Agriculture to Reduce Pesticide Use* (Washington, DC: Natural Resources Defense Council, May 1991), and Miguel Altieri, *Agroecology: The Scientific Basis of Alternative Agriculture* (Boulder, CO: Westview Press, 1987).

129. See, for example, Candace Siegle, "Organic Farming Grows Profits," *Business Mexico*, Dec. 1990. The recent creation of the Mexican Association of Ecological Farmers also points to the expanded market for organic produce in Mexico.

130. Monica Moore, "GATT, Pesticides, and Democracy," *Global Pesticide Campaigner* 1, no. 1 (Oct. 1990):13.

131. Testimony introduced by Sen. Patrick Leahy (D-VT), Sen. Albert Gore (D-TN), and Rep. Mike Synar (D-OK) before the U.S. Senate Agricultural Committee on the Pesticide Export Reform Act, 28 March 1990.

132. Ernst Feder, *El imperialismo fresa: Una investigación sobre los mecanismos de la dependencia en la agricultura Mexicana* (Mexico, D.F.: Ediciones Campesino, 1976).

133. See Iván Restrepo, *Naturaleza muerta: Los plaguicidas en México* (Mexico, D.F.: Centro de Ecodesarrollo, 1988), and the *Boletín de la Red de Acción sobre Plaguicidas y Alternativas en México*, ed. Fernando Bejarano (Mexico, D.F.).

134. Interview with Catalina Denman, professor at El Colegio de Sonora, 6 Feb. 1991.

135. Luis Marco del Pont, "Contaminación en alimentos y consequencias," in Marcos López Torres, ed., *Envenamiento* (Ciudad Juárez: Escuela Superior de Agricultura, 1991), 99.

136. Interview with Calleros (see n. 27).

137. Such an inventory, however, had been compiled in 1991 for at least one state, Baja California. Hazardous wastes generally refer to those that are corrosive, reactive, flammable, or toxic (determined by various tests). Acids, bases, liquids and solids containing heavy metals, metal-plating wastes, organic and inorganic solvents, and cyanide wastes are examples of commonly generated hazardous wastes. For an excellent study see the Texas Center for Policy Studies' *Overview of Environmental Issues* (n. 97).

138. Whereas Mexico bans hazardous waste imports for dumping or incineration, it does allow imported wastes to be recycled or otherwise reused. The EPA registered nineteen hazardous waste shipments to Mexico in 1991.

139. Howard Applegate and C. Richard Bath, "Hazardous and Toxic Substances in U.S.-Mexico Relations," *Texas Business Review* 57, 1983.

140. Center for Investigative Reporting and Bill Moyers, *Global Dumping Ground: The International Traffic in Hazardous Waste* (Washington, DC: Seven Locks Press, 199), 52.

141. Ibid., citing William Carter of the Los Angeles District Attorney's Office.

142. Sgt. Lance Erickson cited in *Los Angeles Times*, 9 May 1990.

143. Cited in Sarah Henry, "The Poison Trail," *Los Angeles Times*, 23 Sept. 1990.

144. Ron Chepesiuk, "From Ash to Cash: The International Trade in Toxic Waste," *E Magazine*, July 1991.

145. For an overview of the problem and international and national efforts to control it, see Mary Tieman, "Waste Exports: U.S. and International Efforts to Control Transboundary Movement," *CRS Issue Brief* (Washington, DC: Congressional Research Service, 20 Aug. 1992).

146. Chepesiuk, "From Ash to Cash" (see n. 144).

147. See Diane Perry et al., "Binational Management of Hazardous Waste: The Maquiladora Industry at the U.S.-Mexico Border," *Environmental Management* 14, no. 4:441.

148. Sanford J. Lewis, Marco Kaltofen, and Mary Waygan, *Border Trouble: Rivers in Peril* (Boston: National Toxic Campaign Fund, May 1991).

149. *Improved Monitoring and Enforcement Needed for Toxic Pollutants Entering Sewers* (Washington, DC: General Accounting Office, April 1989).

150. *Notices of Intent to Import Hazardous Waste* (Washington, DC: Environmental Protection Agency, 1989).

151. Bruce Tomaso and Richard Alm, "Economy vs. Ecology: Toxic Wastes from Border Plants Poorly Monitored," *Transboundary Resources Report*, Spring 1990.

152. Gregory Gross, "Accountability Trail Ends, But Toxic Stream Rolls On," *San Diego Union*, 16 June 1991.

153. *Hazardous Waste: Management of Maquiladora's Waste Hampered by Lack of Information* (Washington, DC: General Accounting Office, Feb. 1992), 3.

154. Ibid.

155. Gross, "Accountability Trail Ends" (see n. 152).

156. Ibid.

157. For a description of the hazardous waste problem in Mexico, particularly as it relates to the maquiladoras, see Roberto A. Sánchez, "Health and Environmental Risks of the Maquiladora in Mexicali," *Natural Resources Journal* 30 (Winter 1990):163-86.

158. *San Diego Union-Tribune*, 14 March 1992.

159. Cody, "Expanding Waste Line" (see n. 83).

160. Patrick J. McDonnell, "Mexicans Fear Plant Could Cause 'Next Bhopal,' " *Los Angeles Times*, 20 Nov. 1991.

161. Mary E. Kelly, *A Response to the Bush Administration's Environmental Action Plan for Free Trade Negotiations with Mexico* (Austin: Texas Center for Policy Studies, May 1991), 12.

162. Roberto A. Sánchez, "Environment: Mexican Perspective," in Sidney Weintraub, ed., *U.S.-Mexican Industrial Integration: The Road to Free Trade* (Boulder, CO: Westview Press, 1991), 311.

163. Statement of the National Safe Workplace Institute, United States Free Trade Hearings, 6 and 20 Feb. 1991, 374-75. Also see Rafael Moure-Eraso et al., *Back to the Future: Sweatshop Conditions of the Mexico-U.S. Border* (Lowell, MA: University of Lowell Work Environment Program, 21 May 1991).

164. Joseph LaDou, "Deadly Migration," *Technology Review* 94, no. 5 (July 1991):50.

165. Mexican laws—Ley Federal del Trabajo and the Ley General de Salud—have established measures to protect workers, but as Sánchez has observed, in practice these laws are largely unenforced. Sánchez, "Environment: Mexican Perspective," in Weintraub, *U.S.-Mexican Industrial Integration*, 308 (see n. 162).

166. See the studies of Catalina A. Denman, professor at El Colegio de Sonora, including "Tiempos Modernos: Trabajar y Morir," paper presented at a roundtable sponsored by the Friedrich Ebert Foundation, 6 and 7 Nov. 1989, Hermosillo, Sonora, and her master's thesis, "Repercusiones de la industria maquiladora de exportación en la salud: El peso al nacer de hijos de obreras en Nogales," Colegio de Sonora, 1988.

167. Leslie Kochan, *The Maquiladoras and Toxics: The Hidden Costs of Production South of the Border* (Washington, DC: AFL-CIO, Feb. 1989), 11.

168. See Steve Fox, *Toxic Work* (Philadelphia: Temple University Press, 1991).

169. "The Impact on Women's Health of the Maquiladoras: The Tijuana Case," *Carnegie Quarterly* 36 (Fall 1991):14. According to the director of the study, Sylvia Guendelman, "The results suggest that, when compared with other risks in the community closely related to a poor lifestyle, the adverse effects of maquiladoras, previously reported in the literature, seem to have been exaggerated."

170. Sánchez, "Environment: Mexican Perspective," in Weintraub, *U.S.-Mexican Industrial Integration*, 308 (see n. 162).

171. David J. Molina, "A Comment on Whether Maquiladoras Are in Mexico for Low Wages or to Avoid Pollution Abatement Costs," *Journal of Environment and Development* 2, no. 1 (Winter 1993).

172. Alejandro Mercado, José Negrete, and Roberto Sánchez, *Capital internacional y relocalización industrial en la Frontera Norte de México* (Tijuana: COLEF, 1989).

173. "Although relocation of investment to avoid stricter environmental restrictions may be a plausible outcome of differences in environmental standards and enforcement, and such movement has taken place in some instances, the phenomenon does not appear to be widespread, nor is it likely to characterize the formation of a NAFTA. This is because relatively few firms meet all of the conditions required for profitable pollution-haven investment—high environmental compliance costs, a big change in locational incentives as a result of removal of trade barriers, low costs associated with new investment, and actual differences in environmental standards." The study concluded that looser pollution enforcement in Mexico would not encourage a systematic transfer of investment because pollution control equipment is such a small share of production costs (averaging 1.1 percent) and that for the industries with the highest pollution control costs, like the chemical industry, Mexican tariffs are low already and these industries are capital-intensive, making relocation costs extremely high. *Review of U.S.-Mexico Environmental Issues*, report prepared by an interagency task force coordinated by the Office of the U.S. Trade Representative (Washington, DC, Feb. 1992),

171. For a supporting position, see Christopher Duerksen, *Environmental Regulation of Industrial Plant Siting: How to Make It Work Better* (Washington, DC: Conservation Foundation, 1983). It should be noted, however, that although *relocation* costs are prohibitive for highly capital intensive industries, such as chemical production, the decision of where to locate *new* investment is much more easily affected by the expected costs of pollution control and occupational safety measures.

174. A survey by the Colegio de la Frontera Norte in Tijuana did, however, show that environmental factors were significant. About 10 percent of the maquiladoras surveyed cited environmental regulations as a primary factor in the decision to leave the United States, and 17 percent considered environmental regulations an important factor. Mercado et al., *Capital internacional* (see n. 172).

175. See Barry Castleman, "How We Export Dangerous Industries," *Business and Society Review* (Fall 1978), 7-14, and Stephen P. Mumme, "Complex Interdependence and Hazardous Waste Management along the U.S.-Mexico Border," in Charles E. Davis and James P. Lester, eds., *Dimensions of Hazardous Waste Politics and Policy* (New York: Greenwood Press, 1988), 227. Mumme observes that export-oriented firms employing toxins in the production process have taken advantage of lax regulation in Mexico, including several asbestos manufacturers and industries using carcinogenic substances like lindane, chlordane, polychlorinated biphenyls, trichloroethylene, and hydrochloric acid.

176. See, for example, Michael G. Royston, "Control by Multinational Corporations: The Environmental Case for Scenario 4," *Ambio* 4, no. 2-3 (1979):84-89. An interesting twist is that large foreign corporations probably have an advantage over many domestic firms in meeting environmental regulations given their accumulated experience and access to technology. See Charles S. Pearson, "Environmental Standards, Industrial Relocation, and Pollution Havens," in Pearson, *Multinational Corporations*, 120 (n. 109). Pearson even suggests that "the combination of in-house technology, expertise, and prior experience—all intangible assets that form the basis of the monopolistic advantage theory—suggest that the introduction of environmental regulations in developing countries will promote foreign investment, not block it."

177. Pearson, *Multinational Corporations*, 123 (see n. 109), and Gabriele Knodgen, "Environment and Industrial Siting: Results of an Empirical Survey of Investment by West German Industry in Developing Countries," *Zeitschrift für Umweltpolitik*, no. 2 (1979).

178. See Gene M. Grossman and Alan B. Krueger, "Environmental Impacts of a North American Free Trade Agreement," discussion paper no. 158 (Princeton: Woodrow Wilson School, Princeton University, Feb. 1992); Mumme, "Complex Interdependence," in Davis and Lester, *Hazardous Waste Politics and Policy* (n. 175); Christopher Duerksen and H. Jeffrey Leonard, "Environmental Regulations and the Location of Industries: An International Perspective," *Columbia Journal of World Business* (Summer 1982); and Castleman, "How We Export Dangerous Industries" (n. 175). Also see H. Jeffrey Leonard, *Are Environmental Regulations Driving U.S. Industry Overseas?* (Washington, DC: The Conservation Foundation, 1984), in which Leonard concludes that although there has been some migration to Mexico of hazardous industries (especially asbestos and building supplies manufacturing) and nonferrous metal smelting and refining, factors unrelated to workplace health and safety and to pollution control costs were largely responsible for the new investment in Mexico.

179. International Labor Office, *Safety and Health Practices of Multinational Enterprises* (Geneva, 1984), 58-59. At the same time, however, Mexican authorities viewed the health and safety performance of the TNCs as being superior to that of domestically owned operations.

180. Gerald V. Poje and Daniel M. Horowitz, *Phantom Reductions: Tracking Toxic Trends* (Washington, DC: National Wildlife Federation, 1990).

181. See *U.S.-Mexico Trade: Some U.S. Wood Furniture Firms Relocated from Los Angeles Area to Mexico* (Washington, DC: General Accounting Office, April 1991). The report notes that not all industry flight from the Los Angeles area has been to Mexico. Seeking to escape the emissions regulations of the South Coast region, companies have also moved to northern California and to southern states such as Georgia where environmental compliance costs are low.

182. Judy Pasternak, "Firms Find a Haven from U.S. Environmental Rules," *Los Angeles Times*, 19 Nov. 1991.

183. Cited in LaDou, "Deadly Migration," 50 (see n. 164).

184. *Comercio Exterior* 41, no. 9 (Sept. 1991):863. The furniture industry ranks fourth in the number of plants and sixth in the number of employees.

185. Robert Reinhold, "Mexico Proclaims an End to Sanctuary for Polluters," *New York Times*, 18 April 1991.

186. During the 1976-1990 period, the lime plant had no U.S. ownership, but in 1991 Sonocal was purchased by the Texas-based firm Chemstar.

187. Dick Kamp, "Lime Dust in My Children's Lungs," testimony before the EPA, 26 Sept. 1991, Nogales, Arizona.

188. See Jan Gilbreath, "Financing Environmental and Infrastructure Needs on the Texas-Mexico Border: Will the Mexican-U.S. Integrated Border Plan Help?" *Journal of Environment and Development* 1, no. 1 (Summer 1992):151-75, for a discussion of these ideas.

189. For an interesting examination of the U.S. section of the IBWC and its special status among U.S. government agencies, see Stephen P. Mumme, "Regional Power in National Diplomacy: The Case of the U.S. Section of the International Boundary and Water Commission," *Journal of Federalism* 14, no. 4 (Fall 1984). Also see Mumme, "Engineering Diplomacy" (n. 13).

190. The IBWC is responsible for a wide range of administrative and operational duties relating to boundary questions and water resources along the border. These include: resolving boundary disputes; maintaining stable river boundaries; maintaining bridges and other structures that cross the boundary; distributing the waters of the Rio Grande/Rio Bravo and the Colorado River between the two countries; jointly operating international dams; sponsoring joint flood control operations; monitoring water quality; designing and constructing water and wastewater treatment plants; resolving water quality problems, including excessive salinity resulting from U.S. agricultural irrigation; and maintaining surface water reservoirs.

191. This Memorandum of Understanding committed the EPA and Mexico's Subsecretaria de Mejoramiento del Ambiente and its head agency, the Secretaría de Salud y Asistencia, to a "cooperative effort to resolve environmental protection matters of mutual concern in border areas as well as any environmental protection matters through exchanges of information and personnel, and the establishment of parallel projects which the two parties consider appropriate to adopt." Quoted in Stephen P. Mumme and Joseph Nalven, "National Perspectives on Managing Transboundary Environmental Hazards: The U.S.-Mexico Border Region," *Journal of Borderlands Studies* 3, no. 1 (Spring 1988).

192. A 1980 Joint Marine Pollution Contingency Plan built on the 1978 memorandum and committed the two countries to cooperate on offshore pollution problems such as oil spills. Several other agreements were concluded in the following years.

193. Eight agreements were signed between 1983 and early 1992: Framework Agreement on Cooperation for Protection and Improvement of the Environment, Annexes I, II, III, IV, and V (1983); Bilateral Agreement for Protection of the Environment along the Border (1983); Agreement for the Conservation of Wildlife (1983); Memorandum of Understanding between Mexico and the United States for the Creation of a Joint Com-

mittee on Wild Plant and Animal Life (1988); Memorandum of Understanding for the Creation of the Committee on Protected Areas in Mexico and the United States (1988); Cooperation Agreement for Environmental Protection and Improvement in the Mexico City Metropolitan Area (1989); Agreement to Improve the Quality of Air in Mexico City and Its Metropolitan Area (1990); and the Integrated Environmental Plan for the Mexican-U.S. Border Area, First Stage, 1992-1994 (1992).

194. For a description of SEDUE's administrative structure and functional responsibilities, see Stephen P. Mumme, C. Richard Bath, and Valerie J. Assetto, "Political Development and Environmental Policy in Mexico," *Latin American Research Review* 23, no. 1 (1988).

195. There are a number of excellent reports by experts on environmental degradation and environmental policy that examine the flaws summarized here. These reports include: Kelly, *Facing Reality* (see n. 66); Jan Gilbreath Rich, *Planning the Border's Future: The Mexican-U.S. Integrated Border Environmental Plan*, U.S.-Mexican Occasional Paper No. 1 (Austin: U.S.-Mexican Policy Studies Program, University of Texas at Austin, March 1992); Michael Gregory, "Environment, Sustainable Development, Public Participation and the NAFTA: A Retrospective," *Journal of Environmental Law and Litigation* 7 (Aug. 1992, prepublication draft).

196. The economic crisis strangled funding for SEDUE. According to Javelly Girard, secretary of SEDUE from 1983 to 1985, "The selective credit policy of the [central] Bank of Mexico has not directed revenues to ecology, and for that reason we lack the instruments necessary to fight pollution." Quoted in Francisco Garfias, "Faltan recursos financieros para combatir la contaminación: Javelly," *Excélsior*, 16 Nov. 1984, A4.

197. In comparison, the United States spends about $24 per person on environmental programs.

198. Even before NAFTA negotiations opened, the Salinas government enhanced environmental protection activities because of public pressure and the need to win back voter support for PRI after the 1988 elections. These enforcement actions were described by one U.S. critic as "demonstration projects" designed to "preempt" independent efforts at reform. Stephen P. Mumme, "System Maintenance and Environmental Reform in Mexico: Salinas's Preemptive Strategy," *Latin American Perspectives* 19, no. 1 (Winter 1992):18.

199. See, for example, "A Response to the EPA/SEDUE Integrated Border Environment Plan" (Austin: Texas Center for Policy Studies, 1 March 1992); Gregory, "Environment, Sustainable Development, Public Participation and the NAFTA" (n. 195); Kelly, "Facing Reality" (n. 66); and Gilbreath Rich, *Planning the Border's Future* (n. 195).

200. Environmental activists roundly criticized the IBWC's continuing authority over border water pollution even though the body's treaty status gives its agreements extra weight compared with accords reached through other agencies. Despite its mandate, the commission has moved slowly to resolve sewage and pollution questions along the border. It is reluctant to use its access to the courts to enforce its agreements, relying upon the U.S. and Mexican governments to enforce their own standards for water quality and pollution cleanup. Activists believe that the IBWC neglects to consult with local organizations and communities about their concerns and the impacts of IBWC public works on local environments. Analysts have faulted the agency for operating behind closed doors and for being an unrepresentative, appointed body. See, for instance, Gregory, "Environment, Sustainable Development, Public Participation and the NAFTA," 75-76 (n. 195), and Gilbreath Rich, "Bordering on Trouble," 32 (n. 38).

201. Quoted in Patrick McDonnell, "Environmental Fears Voiced on Free-Trade Plan," *Los Angeles Times*, 24 Sept. 1991, B2

202. See: Gregory, "Environment, Sustainable Development, Public Participation and the NAFTA" (n. 195); Stewart Hudson, *Comments on the Draft Review of the U.S.-Mexico Environmental Issues* (Washington, DC: National Wildlife Federation, n.d.); Justin

Ward and Lynn Fischer, *Comments on the Draft Review of U.S.-Mexico Environmental Issues* (Washington, DC: Natural Resources Defense Council, Grupo de los Cien, and Instituto Autonomo de Investigaciones Ecologicas, Dec. 1991); and Michael McCloskey and John Audley, *Concerns Arising out of the Environmental Review on NAFTA* (Washington, DC: Sierra Club, 29 Nov. 1991).

203. Interview with Lynn Fischer, 3 Aug. 1992.

204. Much of the following discussion is drawn from a paper by Anne L. Alonzo, *Mexico* (Mexico, D.F.: U.S. Embassy, Feb. 1992). Alonzo is the EPA's environmental attaché in Mexico City.

205. The latter task fulfills more than environmental purposes. It also will facilitate increased trade in pesticides between the two countries.

206. SEDESOL took over environmental policy formulation and enforcement, urban planning, and administration of the National Solidarity Program (Pronasol). It also included the National Indigenous Institute. *Mexico Environmental Issues: Fact Sheets* (Washington, DC: Mexican Embassy, n.d.) and Edward M. Ranger Jr. and Anne Alonzo, "SEDUE Re-emerges under SEDESOL," *Business Mexico*, Sept. 1992.

207. *Mexico Environmental Issues*, 13-14 (ibid.).

208. David Clark Scott, "Mexico Shake-up Rattles Environmentalists," *Christian Science Monitor*, 4 May 1992, 6.

209. Interview with Mario Aguilar, 27 July 1992.

210. Dick Kamp, letter to Charles Ries regarding the Draft Environmental Review of NAFTA, 11 Dec. 1991.

211. Rosa Ma. Chavarria Diaz, "Elimina SEDUE al 48% de los inspectores que verificaban empresas contaminantes," *El Nacional*, 11 Nov. 1991.

212. *U.S.-Mexico Trade: Assessment of Mexico's Environmental Controls for New Companies* (Washington, DC: General Accounting Office, Aug. 1992).

213. Noting the need for enhanced monitoring efforts, these two organizations issued a draft report summarizing environmental problems reported in news articles and other documents. Proyecto Fronteriza de Educación Ambiental and Border Ecology Project, *The North American Free Trade Agreement: Environmental and Health Issues in the Interior of Mexico and Options for Environmental Safeguards*, working draft (Naco, AZ, 8 Oct. 1992). Other groups monitoring border environmental and health conditions and devising programs to respond to them are the Ambos Nogales Project and the Northeast Sonora–Cochise County Health Council. Both are binational working groups with grassroots origins composed of representatives from local health agencies, nongovernmental organizations, community groups, and government agencies.

214. *World Bank Staff Appraisal* (see n. 4).

215. Diane Lindquist, "U.S., Mexico Plan Pact on Environment: NAFTA Critics' Concerns to Be Addressed," *San Diego Union-Tribune*, 22 Sept. 1992.

216. William F. Joffrey cited in Roberto Suro, "Border Boom's Dirty Residue Imperils U.S.-Mexico Trade," *New York Times*, 31 March 1991.

217. Co-optive tactics, often complemented by more repressive measures for intractable critics, have long been practiced by the PRI. Title V of Mexico's 1988 General Law on the environment includes provisions for "social participation," in the form of consultations with sectors such as labor, business, peasants, academics, and NGOs. Another section of the law provides that citizens can denounce violations of environmental laws to Mexican authorities and requires an official investigative report and action brief within thirty days of the complaint. These provisions sound good on paper, but in practice, participation has been open primarily to groups that favor the PRI and its environmental policies. In other cases, environmental militants from groups like the Pacto de Ecologistas have been solicited into the government and their criticisms thereby quieted. Those groups that have remained sharply critical of the government's

policies have complained of being excluded from government-sponsored forums on environmental issues. Others, such as the prominent Group of 100, have accused the Salinas government of more actively quashing dissent with methods such as censorship and harassment. See Mumme, "System Maintenance," 123-43 (n. 198).

218. "United States Environmental Protection Agency Advisory Committee Charter: EPA Border Environmental Plan Public Advisory Committee" (Washington, DC: Environmental Protection Agency, n.d.)

219. Interview with Gail Sevrens, Border Progress Foundation, 23 July 1992. Altogether the EPA granted $150,000 to the foundation in its first two years.

220. Sal Drum, "The Final Plan: A Blueprint for Border Environmental Improvement," *Maquila Magazine*, April 1992.

221. See, for example, Proyecto Fronteriza de Educación Ambiental and Border Ecology Project, *The North American Free Trade Agreement* (n. 213), and Gregory, "Environment, Sustainable Development, Public Participation and the NAFTA" (n. 195).

222. In addition to new environment/trade issues being raised, trade negotiators are being forced to reconcile trade and environmental issues with respect to such international agreements as the Montreal Protocol on Substances that Deplete the Ozone Layer, the Basel Convention on the Control of the Transboundary Movement of Hazardous Wastes and Their Disposal (still awaiting the consent of the U.S. Senate), and the 1973 Convention on the International Trade in Endangered Species, which imposes strict trade controls on species that would otherwise become endangered and bans trade in species that are endangered.

223. See two excellent reports published by the Congressional Research Service: *Environment and Trade* (Washington, DC, 15 Nov. 1992) and *International Environmental Issues: Overview* (Washington, DC, 27 July 1992).

224. The convening of GATT's environmental committee was the direct result of a request by the European Free Trade Association reflecting rising concerns in Europe about the effect of free trade on national environmental and consumer law.

225. In the wake of unfavorable U.S. reaction, Mexico indicated that it was asking for a postponement of a final GATT ruling, but other tuna-exporting countries still pushed for a final judgment on this precedent-setting trade ruling.

226. In his 1 May 1991 Action Plan aimed at swaying environmental and, to a lesser extent, labor critics of the fast-track NAFTA negotiations, President Bush said that some environmental concerns would be treated within the agreement itself while also promising that labor and environmental issues would be addressed more thoroughly in initiatives that would run "in parallel with" the actual negotiations. The first examples of this parallel track were the Integrated Border Environmental Plan and the Environmental Review of U.S.-Mexico Environmental Issues, both of which were released in Feb. 1992. Bush also included representatives of a few environmental organizations on the working groups that advised U.S. NAFTA negotiators, but he declined to create a working group specifically on the environment.

227. The Sierra Club and Public Citizen have argued that a zero tolerance regulation could be challenged under NAFTA because of the agreement's requirement that standards be consistent among the three countries.

228. See Chapter Twenty of NAFTA, "Institutional Arrangements and Dispute Settlement Procedures," especially Articles 2001, 2016, and 2017.

229. Lori Wallach, "The NAFTA Does Not Measure Up on the Environment and Consumer Health and Safety" (Washington, DC: Public Citizen, 1992).

230. Rather than relying on economic growth to create the needed revenues for environmental protection and enforcement, national environmental organizations such as the Sierra Club, the Natural Resources Defense Council, and the Environmental Defense Fund have proposed a variety of directed revenue-generating measures. Adhering to

the "polluter should pay" principle, some propose that corporations investing in Mexico turn over a percentage of their profits to an environmental protection fund or that a "green tax" be levied on cross-border trade. It has also been suggested that countries collect pollution control bonds from industrialists and that countervailing duties be imposed on goods manufactured employing environmentally destructive practices.

231. Robert B. Zoellick of the U.S. Department of State, in testimony before the U.S. Senate Committee on Foreign Relations, "North American Free Trade Agreement: Extending Fast Track Negotiating Authority," 102nd Cong., 1st sess., 11 April 1991. The Salinas administration apparently attempted to bolster this line of attack. A major daily newspaper in Mexico, *Excelsior,* ran a front-page story on 27 Dec. 1992 reporting that a prestigious group of Mexican environmentalists had accused U.S. environmental groups of using "pseudo-environmentalist arguments" and "tendentious propaganda" to "manipulate" public opinion in opposition to free trade. Had the story been true, it would have represented a significant blow to U.S. groups, who count on the support of their Mexican counterparts to overcome right-wing accusations that environmental measures are merely disguised protectionism. The organization quoted by *Excelsior,* however, immediately denied having made any such accusations. Homero Aridjis, head of the environmentalist Group of 100, accused the Mexican government of planting the story in an effort to influence the upcoming meeting between Salinas and U.S. President-elect Clinton, at which NAFTA was topic number one. Ethel Riquelme, "Argumentos Seudoecologistas Manipulan en EU: Los 100," *Excelsior,* 27 Dec. 1992, 1, and interview with Geoffrey Land, Border Ecology Project, 21 Jan. 1993.

232. Francisco Lara, director of the Colegio de la Frontera Norte in Nogales, Sonora, quoted in Marc Levinson, "The Green Gangs," *Newsweek,* 3 Aug. 1992.

233. See John Cavanagh et al., *Trading Freedom: How Free Trade Affects our Lives, Work, and Environment* (San Francisco: Institute for Food and Development Policy, 1992).

234. Testimony of Lori Wallach before the U.S. House of Representatives Committee on Foreign Affairs, Economic Policy and Trade Subcommittee and the Western Hemisphere Subcommittee, 9 Dec. 1991.

235. This definition is drawn from the 1987 report of the World Commission on Environment and Development, *Our Common Future* (Brundtland Commission).

236. This definition is taken from Michael Gregory, "Sustainable Development vs Economic Growth: Environmental Protection as an Investment in the Future," statement before the International Trade Commission, *Hearing on the Probable Economic Effect of a Free Trade Agreement between the United States and Mexico,* 8 April 1991.

237. For a summary of this viewpoint see Wesley R. Smith, "Protecting the Environment in North America with Free Trade," *Heritage Foundation Backgrounder,* 2 April 1992.

238. Gregory, "Environment, Sustainable Development, Public Participation and the NAFTA" (see n. 195).

239. For such a proposal see Alan Neff, "Not in Their Backyards Either: A Proposal for a Foreign Environmental Practices Act," *Ecology Law Quarterly,* no. 471 (1990). Neff, of the Chicago Corporation Commission, proposed the establishment of a U.S. Foreign Environmental Practices Act, modeled after the Foreign Corrupt Practices Act, which could be attached to the Securities Exchange Act of 1934. Under this proposal U.S. corporations and citizens would be subject to both criminal and civil prosecution in U.S. courts for violating applicable U.S. environmental laws and regulations abroad.

Selected Environmental Organizations

The environmental organizations listed below are among the most active in bilateral environmental and public-health issues. For a more complete listing, see the Resource Center's *Cross-Border Links: A Directory of Organizations in Canada, Mexico, and the United States* (1992) or consult the Resource Center's Cross-Border Clearinghouse, which is a database containing more than a thousand organizations and contacts along the border. Many of the following organizations are also members of much broader citizen networks including numerous local groups.

Arizona Toxics Information
PO Box 1896
Bisbee, AZ 85603
Phone: (602) 432-7340
Fax: (602) 432-7340
Contact: Michael Gregory

Binational Health and Environment Coalition of Ambos Nogales
c/o Rural Health Office, University of Arizona
2501 E. Elm St.
Tucson, AZ 85716
Phone: (63) 13-04-26 (Sonora); (602) 626-7946 (Arizona)
Fax: (602) 326-6429
Contact: Ricardo Carrasco (Sonora) or Jean McClelland (Arizona)

Binational Network
c/o Bioconservación
A.P. 504
San Nicolás de la Garza, N.L. 66450
Phone: (83) 76-22-31
Contact: Salvador Contreras Balderas

Border Ecology Project
PO Drawer CP
Bisbee, AZ 85603
Phone: (602) 432-7456
Fax: (602) 432-7473
Contact: Dick Kamp or Geoffrey Land

Coalition for Justice in the Maquiladoras
3120 W. Ashby
San Antonio, TX 78228
Phone: (210) 732-8957
Fax: (210) 732-8324
Contact: Susan Mika

Comité Cívico de Divulgación Ecológica
Madero 1117, Col. Nueva
Mexicali, B.C.
Phone: (65) 52-20-80
Fax: (65) 52-98-12
U.S. mailing address: PO Box 1094, Calexico, CA 92231
Contact: Fernando Medina Robles

Despacho Obrero
Isaac Newton 936
Col. Del Futuro
Ciudad Juárez, Chih.
Phone: (16) 18-43-77
Contact: Gustavo de la Rosa Hickerson

Environmental Committee of the Tijuana-San Diego Region
U.N. Building
Balboa Park
San Diego, CA 92101
Phone: (66) 86-36-87 (Tijuana); (619) 285-9432 (San Diego)
Contact: José Luis Morales (Tijuana) or Kaare S. Kjos (San Diego)

Environmental Health Coalition
1717 Kettner Blvd. Ste #100
San Diego, CA 92101
Phone: (619) 235-0281
Fax: (619) 232-3670
Contact: Diane Takvorian or José Bravo

Pesticide Action Network North America Regional Center
116 New Montgomery Street, Room 810
San Francisco, CA 94105
Phone: (415) 541-9140
Fax: (415) 541-9253
Contact: Monica Moore

Red de Acción sobre Plaguidicas y Alternativas en México (RAPAM)
Vestibulo 57, Colonia Alpes
Mexico, DF CP 01010
Phone: 593-7649
Fax: 660 89 94
Contact: Fernando Bejerano

Red Fronteriza de Salud y Ambiente
c/o El Colegio de Sonora
Av. Obregón 54
Hermosillo, Son. 83000
Phone: (62) 12-65-51/50-21
Contact: Catalina Denman

Texas Center for Policy Studies
PO Box 2618
Austin, TX 78701
Phone: (512) 474-0811
Fax: (512) 478-8140
Contact: Mary Kelly

About the Authors

Tom Barry has been a senior analyst at the Inter-Hemispheric Education Resource Center since its founding in 1979. He is a co-author of *The Great Divide: The Challenge of U.S.-Mexico Relations in the 1990s* (Grove Press, forthcoming) and is the author or co-author of all the books in the Resource Center's *Country Guide* series. He is the author of *Central America Inside Out* (Grove Weidenfeld, 1991), co-author of *Feeding the Crisis* (University of Nebraska Press, 1991), and author of *Roots of Rebellion* (South End Press, 1986).

Beth Sims, a research associate at the Inter-Hemispheric Education Resource Center, is the author, co-author, or contributor to several books, including *The Great Divide: The Challenge of U.S.-Mexico Relations in the 1990s*, *Runaway America: U.S. Jobs and Factories on the Move* (Resource Center Press, 1993), *Workers of the World Undermined: American Labor's Role in U.S. Foreign Policy* (South End Press, 1992), and *Mexico: A Country Guide* (Resource Center, 1992). She received her Master's in Political Science from the University of New Mexico.

Resource Center Press

Resource Center Press is the imprint of the Inter-Hemispheric Education Resource Center, a private, non-profit, research and policy institute located in Albuquerque, New Mexico. Founded in 1979, the Resource Center produces books, policy reports, audiovisuals, and other educational materials about U.S. foreign policy, as well as sponsoring popular education projects. For more information and a catalog of publications, please write to the Resource Center, Box 4506, Albuquerque, New Mexico 87196.

Board of Directors

Border
Ecology
Project

Based in Bisbee, Arizona, Border Ecology Project (BEP) is a nonprofit environmental organization conducting research, advocacy, and program coordination on a range of environmental issues affecting the United States and Mexico, with a focus on the border region. The BEP has played a major role in promoting strong environmental and health safeguards under a North American Free Trade Agreement (NAFTA) and other transboundary regimes. The BEP is currently working in close collaboration with nongovernmental environmental organizations, academic institutions, and state and federal governmental agencies in Mexico to institutionalize pilot right-to-know programs in the Mexican border region.

The BEP has published reports, studies, and working papers on transboundary effects of smelter pollution, hazardous materials in the maquiladora industry, and U.S.-Mexico free trade negotiations and the environment. Its most recent publication is *Environmental and Health Issues in the Interior of Mexico: Options for Transnational Safeguards*. For more information, call Dick Kamp (director) or Geof Land (border coordinator) at (602) 432-7456.

Forthcoming from Grove Press, April 1994

The Great Divide

The Challenge of U.S.-Mexico Relations in the 1990s

Tom Barry, Harry Browne, and Beth Sims

""All international borders are at once fascinating and disconcerting . . . But it is not the contrasting cultures . . . that [make] crossing the U.S.-Mexico line so shocking . . . it is the experience of passing so rapidly between economic worlds.**""** — *excerpt*

The Great Divide is an in-depth examination of the U.S.-Mexico relationship—one that has often been volatile, characterized by prejudice, imperialism, and violence, and only recently by cooperation and mutual dependence. This precarious harmony is threatened by the potentially problematic ramifications of the North American Free Trade Agreement, which, if passed, promises to change permanently the nature of the relationship.

Bound as the U.S. and Mexico are by trade, debt, immigration, and the drug war, the economic and social issues that face both countries play out most visibly along the border. Nine thousand people a day cross illegally into the U.S. through the borderlands; 2,000 maquiladora factories spread across the borderlands employ nearly 500,000 Mexicans and yet are subject to virtually no labor or environmental laws; 50 percent of the cocaine and 75 percent of the marijuana smuggled into the U.S. comes through the borderlands; and the pollution in the area is so bad that a section of the Nogales Wash, a borderlands river, recently exploded.

This is another book in the Grove Press series which includes *The Central America Fact Book* and *Central America Inside Out*.

Mexico: A Country Guide

The Essential Source on Mexican Society,
Economy, and Politics

Edited by Tom Barry

One of our best sellers, *Mexico: A Country Guide* is the only comprehensive book about Mexican society, politics, and economy in the 1990s—an invaluable resource for students, academics, and anyone interested in the interrelationship between our two countries. Includes photos, tables and charts, references, and index.

"Easily the best source book on contemporary Mexican society." – Choice: Current Reviews for College Libraries

ISBN: 0-911213-35-X
Paperback, 401 pages, 1992. $14.95
plus $3.00 shipping and handling

BorderLines

A quarterly from the Resource Center focusing on border issues

This quarterly is an extension of the Resource Center's work on its Cross-Border Links project. It examines the dynamics of cross-border relations, highlighting the problems and successes of popular organizations and government agencies in resolving common issues. It also offers investigative reporting and timely policy analysis about Mexico-U.S. relations.

U.S. subscriptions: $10/year, $17/2 years
Foreign subscriptions: $15/year, $27/2 years

Prices subject to change.

Resource Center
Box 4506 / Albuquerque, NM 87196
(505) 842-8288

The U.S.-Mexico Series

On Foreign Soil: Government Programs in U.S.-Mexico Relations

Disagreements and misunderstandings have traditionally characterized the U.S.-Mexico relationship. Since the mid-1980s, however, the two governments have increasingly seen eye to eye on issues ranging from economics to international affairs. Similar economy policy agendas—characterized by neoliberal policies and free trade initiatives—are the foundation of this new mutual understanding. But simmering beneath the improved relations are such intractable issues as immigration, labor mobility, narcotrafficking, economic disparities, and asymmetric trading and investment power. *On Foreign Soil* breaks new ground in examining current U.S.-Mexico foreign relations, while providing an investigative look at the government programs that characterize this fragile new partnership.

No. 2 in the series. ISBN: 0-911213-44-9. 84 pages, paperback, $9.95

Crossing the Line:
Immigrants, Economic Integration, and Drug Enforcement on the U.S.-Mexico Border

Crossing the Line takes a close and current look at the U.S.-Mexico borderlands. It is along a common border that many of the challenges that face the two nations are most acutely felt. The society and economy of the borderlands reflect historic tensions and divisions between the two nations. At the same time, the increasing interdependence of the neighboring countries is most apparent in the border region. The book looks closely at the cross-border problems presented by the northward migration stream, the maquila economy, the booming narcotics trade, and the infrastructure crisis—problems that extend beyond the borderlands to the heart of U.S.-Mexico relations.

No. 3 in the series. ISBN: 0-911213-46-5. 146 pages, paperback, $9.95

For Richer, For Poorer: Shaping U.S.-Mexican Integration

Money and business are integrating North America. More than any other factor, they have brought the United States and Mexico closer together than at any time since the 1917 Mexican Revolution. The two countries' histories as leaders of the industrialized North and the developing South, respectively, make the emerging partnership a highly influential model for the rest of the world. Important sectors in both nations stand to benefit from closer integration, but the neoliberal economic policies that have cleared the way for booming cross-border trade and investment are wreaking havoc on workers, small businesses, and communities across the continent, and forcing people on both sides of the Rio Grande to come to grips with globalization for the first time. *For Richer, For Poorer* explains the nuts and bolts of globalization, the pros and cons of the free trade debate, and alternative strategies to promote a more balanced process of integration that advances workers' rights and the environment as well as business interests.

No. 4 in the series. ISBN: 0-911213-47-3. 100 pages, paperback, $9.95

**Include $3.00 shipping and handling for the first book,
50¢ for each additional. Prices subject to change.**

**Resource Center
Box 4506 / Albuquerque, NM 87196
(505) 842-8288**

Border Ecology Project
Publications

Estimates of Impacts on Agriculture in Sonora, Mexico, from Copper Smelter-Derived Sulphur Dioxide Pollutants, by Wayne Williams, April, 1986 (in English and Spanish). ($10.00)

Hazardous Material Inventory of Agua Prieta, Sonora, Maquiladoras, with Recommendations for U.S./Mexico Transboundary Regulation, June 1988 (in English and Spanish). ($10.00)

Air Pollution and Tree Dieback: Recent Trends in the U.S. and Canada, November, 1988. ($10.00)

Mexico/U.S. Free Trade Negotiations and the Environment: Exploring the Issues, Border Ecology Project/Texas Center for Policy Studies Discussion Paper, January, 1991 (in English and Spanish). ($5.00)

Clean Air Act and Strategies to Mitigate Economic Impacts on Coalfield Communities, 1990. ($5.00)

Environmental and Health Conditions in the Interior of Mexico: Options for Transnational Safeguards, Border Ecology Project and Proyecto Fronterizo de Educacion Ambiental, February, 1993 (in English and Spanish). ($10.00)

Mexican Mining and the World Bank: Environmental Implications of Liberalization and Restructuring, available December, 1993. ($5.00)

Please send orders and correspondence to:

Border Ecology Project
P.O. Drawer CP
Bisbee, AZ 85603
Phone: (602) 432-7456 * Fax: (602) 432-7473